MEZZO GIORNO

SOUTHERN ITALIAN COOKING

FRANCESCO MAZZEI

PHOTOGRAPHY BY YUKI SUGIURA

TO DAD,
MY FIRST SUPPORTER,
MY BIGGEST FAN

MEZZOGIORNO

INTRODUCTION

I WAS ADAMANT I DIDN'T WANT TO BE A CHEF. Growing up I was mainly concerned with how much time I could spend playing football and my career just needed to fit in around that. It was a child's vanity and a conversation with my father that changed things.

Italy is, of course, a nation of food lovers, but the Italians are also pretty style conscious, and at eight years old I went to ask my dad for some sneakers and a pair of Levi jeans. My family's means were limited and with five kids there was no way my father could afford to buy expensive clothes for us all, so he jokingly suggested I get a job. I suppose the drive to succeed has always been in me, because I took him at his word and went to see my uncle, who owned an ice cream shop in our town, where my elder brother Piero worked, and explained that I needed to make some money to buy Levi jeans. 'Come straight from school tomorrow,' said my uncle, 'you can start at 3pm.' And that was that. I worked in the shop every summer for five years, doing anything and everything I was asked to: washing dishes, waiting on customers, and making the ice creams, sorbets, cakes, biscuits and brioche we used to serve in the little *caffè*. It was hard work and long hours and there were times when I hated it, but I earned a lot of money and it could be fun. I was working with my brother and my cousins Gaetano and Celestina and we used to have a laugh and get to know other kids in the area. But I remember thinking that I never, ever wanted to run a *gelateria* or cook in a restaurant.

So it's a bit ironic that I did eventually sign up to catering college – but to the administrative side. I wanted the easy life and at the time I knew that a General Manager job at a hotel was one of the few jobs that would leave me with plenty of spare time for football. Then one summer, a well-known chef from the region came into the *gelateria* and ordered a *mangia e bevi* – a mixture of sorbets piled high with fresh fruits and served in a glass with a spoon and straw so that you can suck up any sorbet that's melted. There was a buzz in the shop and a fuss over who was going to prepare it for him and I volunteered. I remember arranging the different flavours and fruits so meticulously, and once I'd handed him the creation I watched him eat it. He put his spoon down and called me over to the table. 'This is very good,' he said, 'did you make it?' I nodded and he asked what I was planning to do with my life. I explained that I was going to catering college to learn to manage a hotel. I have never forgotten his words: 'Shame. You can see you've got the touch.'

GROWING UP I WAS MAINLY CONCERNED WITH HOW MUCH TIME I COULD SPEND PLAYING FOOTBALL AND MY CAREER JUST NEEDED TO FIT IN AROUND THAT

That afternoon I went home but didn't tell my parents what had happened – they would never have let me become a chef. I went to the college and asked to swap to the *'cucina'* section, but there wasn't any space so the lady on the admissions desk said I would have to give a demonstration to the teachers to earn a place.

Telling my parents I'd made the switch was a bit of a disaster – they were devastated. At that time being a chef in my region was something that was frowned upon; it was considered a last resort, and the lifestyle associated with being a chef had a bad reputation. But I was determined, and as soon as I started, they recognised my passion. I began this amazing journey.

I ran my first restaurant at the age of 18, which was thrilling and challenging and an amazing learning curve, but I left after six months. My father didn't like the people I was dealing with and persuaded me to leave Calabria and move to where the profession was better supported and valued. My girlfriend – now my wife – was studying at university in Rome, so I moved to the capital. In the city centre was the breathtaking Grand Hotel, a top-class hotel and one of the best in Italy. The food they served there was elegant and refined, combining the best of classical Italian cooking with the principles and discipline of classical French, and I became fixated on working there. One day I went to the kitchen door where a huge man called Paolo Moretti emerged in chef's whites: 'What do you want?' he barked. I remember losing my nerve a little but I knew what I wanted so I held his eye and said: 'I'm looking for a job.' He looked at me as if I were a horse, checking to see if I had good teeth and assessing my stamina, but he eventually said: 'Start tomorrow at 8am for a week's trial.' I arrived at 7am and I don't think I saw sunlight for the next six months. I immersed myself in the sights, sounds and smells of that kitchen, and I loved it. It was the start of an obsession, a passion for cooking that has stayed with me and continues to grow.

I've worked in restaurants of all types, I've learned under some great chefs – in Italy, in the UK and abroad, and I've run other kitchens too, but when I think about cooking and the food that I most love to cook, it is the food from where I grew up, from my home region of Calabria, and above all, from the *mezzogiorno* area Calabria is proud to be a part of – the sun-soaked, southern part of Italy's boot, and what some might consider the heart of the Mediterranean, which continues to inspire me and get my own heart beating. *Mezzogiorno* means 'noon'. It means 'half-day', it means 'lunchtime', but it also means 'poor area'. The *mezzogiorno* in Italy is officially made up of eight regions: Abruzzo, Molise, Campania, Calabria, Basilicata, Puglia, Sicilia and Sardinia. Although the term originally came about because the sun is at its strongest in this area at midday, it also refers to the fact that the whole region had an economy heavily reliant on agriculture, which declined greatly after Italy's unification in the 1860s. The decline created an economic and metaphorical divide between the prospering, industrialised northern provinces, and the struggling farmers in the South, and sadly it was a gulf that continued to widen until long after the Second World War, leading to mass emigration and whole towns in the South being abandoned.

But despite all its historical and official classifications, for me the word *mezzogiorno* simply means home. It is evocative not just of a place, but a feeling: the culture of the South; its sun, its warmth, its beaches, its acres of olive groves and citrus trees, its generosity, its pride in tradition, its produce and above all, its food.

The *mezzogiorno*'s troubled economic history dictates that the style of cooking is rooted in the *cucina povera* tradition. *Cucina povera* means 'cooking of the poor' or 'peasant cooking'. The concept can be found in every culture but at its core is the principle of using what is available to you and transforming humble ingredients into more than the sum of their parts. It is a culture based on using ingredients thriftily, stretching them to create meals that are flavoursome yet sustaining; wasting nothing; and preserving food for the leaner times that might be around the corner. It is food for people who work the land and fish its waters but also use them as their larder. It is the cheap cuts of an animal, offal, vegetables, herbs, pulses, and flour to make the daily bread. It is rustic, hearty and rib-sticking (you will quickly discover that pig and the fat the animal provides forms the backbone of much of traditional southern food), but it is also the freshness and lightness of the Mediterranean – food fit for long, hot summer days and balmy nights; the full-flavoured abundance of colourful vegetables, simply baked or grilled fish, and the beautiful grassy olive oils which are thought to keep hearts healthy. Its principles were instilled in me by my mother and my grandmother from the time I could walk and they are at the core of every recipe in this book. In some cases I have adjusted dishes – lightening, refining and adapting them for the way I, and I hope you, like to eat today, but I have never strayed far from the origins or spirit of the traditional recipe.

Throughout the book, I often refer to cuisine of the *mezzogiorno* or to the South in general terms. This is because there are many characteristics of the cooking and food that unite the eight regions, but this is certainly not to dismiss the fact that each of them has its own identity, traditions, recipes and rituals.

THE WORD *MEZZOGIORNO* IS EVOCATIVE NOT JUST OF A PLACE, BUT A FEELING: THE CULTURE OF THE SOUTH

Abruzzo stretches from the high peaks of the Appenines down to the beaches of the Adriatic Sea, over a mostly wild and mountainous terrain. It is also Italy's 'greenest' region and has a rich culinary tradition. Apparently the biggest number of chefs from any region in Italy are Abruzzese and there is a small town in the province of Chieti, called Villa Santa Maria, which is the 'home of Italian chefs'. There has been a cooking school in the town since the sixteenth century and the town's patron saint, San Francesco Caracciolo, is the protector of cooks (every year, his saint's day is celebrated with a festival in their honour). The region is known for the quality of its smoked meats, its mountain-reared lamb and mutton, its pasta, and also its wine. You are no doubt familiar with a couple of them as Montepulciano d'Abruzzo and Trebbiano d'Abruzzo are very popular red wines abroad.

Just south of Abruzzo is Molise. Nature and a deep-rooted value of tradition characterise this region, which is largely undiscovered by visitors. The winding paths of its *tratturi*, the routes trodden by its shepherds as they made their way down from Abruzzo's mountains to Puglia's more verdant fields for their livestock to graze, are a striking and stunning dissection of the hilly landscape. In culinary terms, Molise has fantastic pasta – fresh and dried – and the La Molisana brand is one of the most famous in Italy and widely exported.

Puglia, the heel of Italy's boot, can also be considered its vegetable garden. The fertile, rich soil of the Tavoliere delle Puglia means the quality of its vegetables and olives (and consequently its oils) is unrivalled, and if you turn to page 193 you can read more about them. But it is also one of Italy's most beautiful regions, with a stunning coastline, fringed by golden sandy beaches and rocky cliff faces, and is possibly the region I love the most.

Campania is a land of contrast and craziness. From the seething streets of sprawling Naples, set in the shadows of the gloomy, mysterious Mount Vesuvius, to the spectacular scenery of the Amalfi Coast, with its tumbling cliffs and villages perched among them, to the elegance of Capri, dazzling in its beauty, and fabled for its hedonism, Campania has something for everyone. And in culinary terms, the world will forever be indebted to the region that is home to *spaghetti* and gave us the *pizza margherita* (see page 265). Campania boasts some of the world's juiciest tomatoes, and this is reflected in many of its traditional recipes, but it is also saturated with the heady aromas of its famous Amalfi lemons and other citrus fruits, and proud of its dairy produce, particularly its *mozzarella di bufala* (see page 36). And finally, the Neapolitans are partial to a pastry or two and the region is well known for some of its desserts, the *sfogliatelle* pastries and the *crema di limone* being ones to look out for.

Take the boat west out of Naples, across clear, emerald-green waters, and you'll dock in Sardinia, an island of dazzling white beaches, wild, rugged landscape and an extraordinary abundance of sheep (there are thought to be over 4 million of them!). I fell in love with Sardinia the first time I set eyes on it, and each time I visit I am hugely inspired by the variety of its cuisine and by how much it can surprise me. Sardinia's geographical situation governs much of its culinary heritage. To the west is Spain, to the north is France, to the east is Italy and

to the south is north Africa, and each country has played its part in influencing the style of food you will find on the island. *Fregola*, a type of Sardinian pasta, made in the same way as its north African cousin couscous (also popular on

the island), is one of my favourite ingredients. The nutty flavour of the small durum wheat balls is fantastic and I'm forever experimenting with them. The sheep population means that there is a strong cheese-making culture in Sardinia, it has some of Italy's finest pecorino and all different kinds of ricotta, and its coastline means that the island is blessed with a wide variety of fish species, including some of the most beautiful lobster I have ever tasted.

Like Sardinia, Italy's largest island, Sicilia, is a crossroad of cultures and the bridge between the Mediterranean and much of the South's Moorish heritage. Smoking Stromboli and the towering Mount Etna make for a dramatic first impression yet they are also reminders of Sicily's turbulent history and the resistance and resourcefulness of its people. The exuberance and liveliness of Sicilians as well as their relaxed

THE WORLD WILL FOREVER BE INDEBTED TO CAMPANIA, THE REGION THAT IS HOME TO *SPAGHETTI* AND GAVE US THE *PIZZA MARGHERITA*

attitude to life is reflected in their food. It is a generous cuisine, predominantly based on vegetables, and Sicily is renowned for having some of the most amazing street food in the world. No trip to the island is complete without a wander around Palermo's market stalls to try *arancini* (deep-fried rice balls), *pane ca meusa* (a grilled sandwich with spleen), *panelle* (chickpea fritters) and *sfincione* (a soft pizza-like bread soaked with tomato, onions and spices), all eaten hot in the street. Sicily has a love of all things sweet, and its pastries and candied fruits, particularly its *cannoli* and *cassata*, which I discuss endlessly in the Dolci chapter (pages 208–247) are world-famous.

Basilicata and Calabria used to be the poorest regions in the *mezzogiorno*, and as neighbours the two also share similarities in the kitchen. Like Calabria, Basilicata is the other southern region to enjoy a hint of spice in its food, though the chilli peppers used are generally slightly milder, and above all Basilicata is famous for its sweet peppers – the bright red, thin-fleshed ones from Senise being particularly highly valued for their flavour. Chillies are sliced then added to dishes raw, grilled and preserved in oil, but generally they are hung from long strings and left to dry in the baking heat of the sun. The dried peppers add sweet, smoky notes to dishes, or they can be pounded even further to make a sweet paprika-like powder. Basilicata is also a region rich in vegetables and the amazing red aubergines from Rotonda have been awarded Protected Designation of Origin (PDO) status. They look more like tomatoes and are in fact orange until they ripen fully, with a sharp, spicy flavour. They are the only ones grown in the world and in Italy can only be cultivated in Rotonda.

And finally there is Calabria, the toe of Italy's boot, and the place where I was born – in a small town called Cerchiara, in the province of Cosenza. Perched on a hillside with the mountains behind and a stunning seaside panorama in front, the drive up to Cerchiara still takes my breath away. My family lived there until I was six, then we moved closer to the seaside to be nearer to my school. We spent weekends in

the countryside with my grandparents in Piana di Cerchiara, and though I never thought of it at the time, it was a childhood that revolved around food. My father's parents had run a monastery in Cerchiara, the Madonna delle Armi. It was well known in the region as the destination for an annual pilgrimage; people travelled for miles to come and see the miracle of the face of the Madonna that had appeared in the stone. But when I was born my grandparents moved back to the countryside. The mountain air around Cerchiara was cold, so they set up home in the milder climate in Piana, which was a fertile area where they had a small farm with pigs, chickens, sheep, rabbits and a vegetable garden. My olive oil still comes from the trees they planted there.

My brothers and I used to help *Nonna* with the cooking, making bread, drying the figs and chillies in her wood-fired oven, harvesting vegetables, looking after the pigs and chickens and making the *salumi*. Like most people in the region, we grew or reared as much of our own food as possible, and absolutely everything we ate was produced ourselves or locally.

My mum's mum died when she was three, and my mother was raised in a convent until she

MY BROTHERS AND I USED TO HELP *NONNA* WITH THE COOKING, MAKING BREAD, DRYING THE FIGS AND CHILLIES IN HER WOOD-FIRED OVEN AND HARVESTING VEGETABLES

was 18. The nuns came from all over Italy, so the cooking she learned from them had lots of different regional influences. Indeed, although when I was a child she generally cooked food that would be considered 'southern', her food had a light touch. She didn't use a lot of pig fat, or much of Calabria's famously fiery chillies, and she cooked mainly with vegetables. And while my grandmother's cooking was more hearty – she would cook a huge pot of borlotti bean soup with a chunk of *guanciale* inside – the soup would be simmered very, very slowly and she would skim off all the fat during the cooking so that it soaked up the beautiful porky flavour without being layered with the heavy fat.

The South was, and still is, a region steeped in tradition, and religion plays a significant role in daily life. My childhood meals were influenced by the Catholic calendar and traditions and they set the rhythm of our week. Sunday was our

feast day and it felt like we never stopped eating, from lunch until dinner. Italians live to eat; if we're not sitting down to a meal we're thinking and talking about the next one, and our lives revolve around food. 'How is the orange season? How are the olives this year? Oh no, the pigs aren't getting fat, should we give them more acorns or more grain?' So although Sunday would start simply, with very dry Cerchiara bread dipped in milk and sugar, conversation would already be focused on lunch: *che vollete mangiare al mezzogiorno?* (what do you want for lunch?). And at lunch it would be, *che mangiamo esta sera?* (what are we having for dinner?).

Sunday lunch would begin with a lot of *antipasti*, which is perhaps the most convivial part of an Italian meal because it's all about sharing. Plates of *salumi*, cheese, *insalata di mare*, pickles and a salad, or several, are passed up and down the table, bottles are opened, glasses are chinked and the feast begins.

Then came the *primo piatto*, which in my house would be not one but two different types of pasta dish. There would usually be a stuffed pasta, such as a *pasta chijna* (see page 96) and a loose one – *alla Norma* or with a meat *ragù*. The bowl would just be set in the middle of the table and everyone would dive in.

Next the lamb, suckling goat, chicken or pork would emerge, usually roasted in the wood-fired oven or grilled on the barbecue. Sometimes we would have a stew – wild boar, or for a special occasion, guinea fowl (see page 144), which would be served with very simple salads – tomatoes or perhaps some *verdure grigliate* (see page 207).

Finally there was dessert: *gelato* which my uncle had given us from the shop, maybe some *pasticcini* (small pastries and biscuits – like petit fours), which Dad would buy from the *pasticceria* for us to share; or sometimes Mum would make *crostata*, a simple tart filled with home-made jam. Then there was a strong *espresso* and, of course, a liqueur to help with digestion – *limoncello* or *bergamello* or *liquorice* or *amaro del capo*, a local bitter digestif.

All this would be followed by a short break – my father would take a nap – and by 5 or 6pm everyone would get dressed up and gather together to go out for the *passeggiata* (early evening stroll) and *gelato* (yes, another!). It felt so natural at that time, but I imagine if you weren't from the area, it must have seemed like such a strange sight – all these people in their smart clothes, sitting on benches or walking along licking ice cream cones. And we weren't the only ones: at that time my uncle's *gelateria* was the only one in Villapiana and I can remember the queue – whatever time you arrived you had to wait.

And so it continued, there was dinner and more feasting. You get the idea, we ate like kings on a Sunday, yet the rest of the week was simple, frugal and always governed by the same rituals: leftovers on Monday, soup on Tuesday, fish on

Wednesday and Friday and just a hint of meat – stretched with breadcrumbs and cheese to make a meal – on Thursdays; something light, a frittata maybe, on Saturdays.

These days, the way Italians eat and enjoy meals is changing. There isn't as much time, or possibly inclination, to have several courses

THESE DAYS, THE WAY ITALIANS EAT AND ENJOY MEALS IS CHANGING; THERE ISN'T AS MUCH TIME TO HAVE SEVERAL COURSES

at each sitting and many people are choosing to have a single dish – a bowl of pasta, say – or only a couple of the courses we used to devour so eagerly. Yet the conviviality and the steadfast belief in the importance of mealtimes, and the joy of sitting down to enjoy food together is still an inherent part of our culture.

The way that I've organised the chapters in the book is based on the traditional format of an Italian meal, for ease of reference rather than through any resolute commitment to tradition. I wanted the book to be simple. I want you to use it how you want, to choose the dishes and do with them what you will to suit the way you cook and eat at home. Make a few of the *antipasti* and serve them alongside a board of *salumi*, have a single pasta dish, swap your Sunday roast for the gratin of slow-cooked lamb shoulder but serve it with traditional British roast potatoes – it's up to you. Above all, I want you to read this book with the same excitement that I have for the *mezzogiorno* and the food that is part of its soul.

My publisher once asked me how I would describe my food. The answer is simple: it's *mamma* cooking with chef's hands. And I want your hands to enjoy making *mamma's* food too. *Buon appetito!*

COOK'S NOTES

I USE EXTRA VIRGIN OLIVE OIL in almost all my cooking but if using it that often is not something that's feasible for you or you can't get hold of a flavour you like, do substitute it with the best-quality olive oil you can afford.

I always, always use dried pulses rather than tinned. I love the ritual involved in soaking pulses the night before use – and it's something I get the kids involved in. In general my recipes need the texture and bulk from the starch that cooking dried pulses brings so I'd urge you to follow the recipe and try soaking and cooking your own.

Garlic and onions are always peeled unless otherwise stated.

Wherever possible I've tried to give you alternatives to the ingredients that are trickiest to source. However, *garum* (anchovy water – see page 123 for a description of what it is) is the ingredient where it's hardest to do this. You can try substituting the oil from a tin of anchovy fillets, but it doesn't always achieve the same result. *Garum* is used in several of the recipes in the book and if you do decide to source it from one of the stockists listed on page 286, it will keep for months, and you can try experimenting with it in other recipes.

In recipes calling for fresh breadcrumbs, I use the insides of a sourdough or rustic Italian loaf, and crumble them up between my hands. If you can do the same you'll be staying true to the recipe's origins but you can, of course, use whatever type of fresh crumb you have available.

In Italy, the *antipasti*, or starter course, will always be a selection of dishes, *salumi* and cheeses and everyone helps themselves to a bit of each. So although I've suggested how many each *antipasto* recipe will serve, I'm assuming that each will be served among several on the table.

The recipes in the Vegetali chapter make good accompaniments to other meat or fish dishes, but the cold ones can also be served as part of an *antipasti*.

ANTIPASTI
E ZUPPE

BURRATA E ARANCIA SANGUINELLA

BURRATA AND BLOOD ORANGE

IF FOOD COULD BE FASHIONABLE, *n'duja* and burrata would currently be top of the A-list's most wanted items. Burrata, meaning 'buttery', is a cheese I grew up with yet it's only quite recently come to the fore in the UK and now I'm constantly seeing it on restaurant menus – Italian or otherwise. It's a beautiful fresh cheese from Puglia made from a mixture of mozzarella and cream. The outside shell, or pouch, is a thin, firm layer of cow's mozzarella; you cut into it to let a liquidy centre of curds and cream spill out. Luxurious yet light – I can't get enough of it.

Here the bitter blood orange has just the right amount of acidity to act as a contrast to the salty, creamy burrata so you don't really feel like you're eating something sweet. The dish is also balanced by one of my favourite bitter leaves, radicchio, which adds another savoury note. It's an unusual combination but I think it works perfectly.

SERVES 4

1 burrata cheese
2½ blood oranges, *peeled, white pith removed, plus the juice of the extra ½*
30g radicchio
30g watercress
30g rocket
2 tsp lemon juice
grated zest of 1 unwaxed lemon
4 tbsp extra virgin olive oil
3 tsp clear honey
30g salted capers, *soaked overnight*
10 hazelnuts, *toasted and chopped*
sea salt and freshly ground black pepper

Leave the burrata at room temperature for 1 hour before starting to prepare the dish.

Cut the blood oranges into thin slices crossways then squeeze the juice of the remaining half into a bowl and set aside.

Place the radicchio, watercress and rocket leaves in a bowl of iced water and set aside. Drain and dry when ready to serve.

Add the lemon juice and zest to the bowl of reserved orange juice, together with the olive oil, honey and some salt and pepper and whisk energetically until nice and creamy.

To serve, open the burrata on to one side of a serving plate, arrange the drained leaves on the other side, then top the leaves with the orange slices and capers. Drizzle with the dressing and finish by scattering the chopped hazelnuts on top.

INSALATA DI FINOCCHI, PUNTARELLE, ARANCE E OLIVE

FENNEL, PUNTARELLE, ORANGE AND OLIVE SALAD

THIS IS BOTH A LIGHT STARTER and a wonderful side dish – a simple assembly of contrasting textures and fresh flavours. Fennel and orange add freshness and acidity, while there's a salty kick from the anchovies and olives. Pile it on to *freselle* (see page 254) if you want to make it more substantial and give it extra crunch.

SERVES 4

½ puntarelle head
1 fennel bulb, *trimmed*
1 large garlic clove, *very finely chopped*
10 tinned anchovies, *very finely chopped*
3 tbsp extra virgin olive oil
2 tbsp red wine vinegar
1 orange, *peeled, white pith removed*
180g pitted black olives
sea salt and freshly ground black pepper

Remove the outer green leaves of the puntarelle to get to the pale green core. Detach each spear, halve and slice thinly lengthways. Put the pieces into iced water and leave them for as long as you can – ideally overnight, but for a few hours at least, until they curl up.

Using a mandolin or sharp knife, slice the fennel very thinly, then add it to the iced water and set aside.

Put the garlic and anchovies into a jug with the olive oil and vinegar and whisk vigorously to make a dressing.

Segment the orange, slicing between the fine membrane to remove the flesh.

Drain the puntarelle curls and fennel and dry thoroughly, then transfer them to a serving bowl and toss with the dressing and some salt and pepper. Finish by scattering over the olives and orange segments.

FRITTATA DI CIPOLLE ROSSE E RICOTTA

RED ONION AND RICOTTA FRITTATA

'FRITTATA', MEANING 'FRIED' is the Italian take on an omelette. It's a fantastic dish that can be eaten at any time of the day, warm out the oven or left to cool then cut into small cubes or chunky wedges for serving with drinks or as an *antipasto*. I like frittata for breakfast but I also associate it with Good Friday – a day of eating for most Italians – as it was something my grandmother always used to prepare for us all to have as a mid-morning snack.

I've deliberately been specific about the type of onion to use. Calabria is famous for its red Tropea onions, which are cultivated all over the region but are particularly sweet when grown in the mild climate by the coast. They're in season from May to July and I really want you to seek them out if you can. If you can't find them, French *griotte* onions or sweet white onions are a good alternative.

SERVES 4

4 Tropea red onions (about 600g), *very finely sliced*
2 tsp extra virgin olive oil
1 tsp caster sugar
1 tbsp white wine vinegar
12 medium eggs
150g pecorino cheese
20g basil leaves
300g fresh ricotta
sea salt and freshly ground black pepper

Preheat the oven to 190°C/fan 170°C/gas 5.

Put the onions and oil into a large ovenproof frying pan over a medium heat with the sugar, vinegar and a pinch of salt. Leave the onions to sweat until they are very soft and transparent. The vinegar will help give them a beautiful crimson colour. Remove from the pan and transfer to a large bowl to cool.

Add the eggs, pecorino, basil and some salt and pepper to the bowl of cooked onions and whisk well. Line the frying pan (there's no need to clean) with oiled baking paper, then pour in the egg mixture. Crumble the ricotta over the top and bake in the oven for 25 minutes or until a strand of spaghetti stuck in the centre comes out clean. Eat warm as your breakfast, lunch or dinner, or leave to cool to room temperature when it will be easy to slice and you can cut it into cubes or wedges to serve as an antipasto.

Clockwise from top left:
provolone del Monaco,
mozzarella di bufala,
burrata, *bocconcini alla*
crema, ricotta.

FORMAGGI

CHEESE

UNLIKE MANY OTHER EUROPEAN COUNTRIES, where cheese is a course in its own right, in Italy it is something we generally associate with the start of a meal (although in Sicily ricotta is used a lot in cakes and pastries, see below and pages 212 and 230). We graze on a small slice or chunk alongside bread and *salumi* with our *aperitivo*; we'll eat it in salad as a starter or as part of an *antipasti* selection. And of course, cheese also adds the essential finishing touch to a steaming bowl of pasta, which is a *primo piatto* (first course). Every region in Italy has its cheeses and most are in some way a reflection of the area's history and geography.

Pecorino is the name given to all cheeses made only from sheep's milk. There are varieties produced all over the country but four have been granted PDO status – pecorino Romano, Sardo, Siciliano and Toscano – and are the ones particularly worth seeking out. Of these, pecorino Romano is undoubtedly the most famous and the most exported. It is one of the oldest cheeses in Italy – as the name implies, it dates from Roman times, and it is still made according to traditional methods, by hand; and in accordance with PDO legislation, it is only allowed to be produced in designated areas: Lazio, Sardinia and the province of Gosseto in Toscano.

Pecorino is aged for a minimum of 5 months, at which point it is considered 'young' or '*fresco*'. At this stage, it is a table cheese, with a rubbery texture and a mild, sweet flavour. Aged for 8–12 months (*stagionato*), the flavour becomes sharper and saltier and at this point it is the cheese we use for grating. While in the North, Parmigiano Reggiano and Grana Padano will be the choice for cooking and for grating over pasta and into risotto, they have long been considered too expensive and in the South we traditionally only use the more humble pecorino.

One of my favourite types of pecorino is *canestrato di Moliterno,* which is made from a mixture of sheep's milk (around 70 per cent) and goat's milk and is produced in the

PECORINO IS THE NAME GIVEN TO ALL CHEESES MADE ONLY FROM SHEEP'S MILK

commune of Moliterno at the intersection of Basilicata, Campania and Calabria. Strictly, the use of goat's milk means it shouldn't be called a pecorino, but in Italy we like to break rules and we all think of it as a true pecorino... In the summer, the animals graze on mountain pasture, which gives the cheese an aromatic, almost fruity flavour. It's a very hard cheese and I like to eat small pieces alongside a glass of red wine, but it's also beautiful grated over pasta.

Piacentinu is another beautiful yet unusual cooked sheep's cheese from Sicily, thought to be named after the local dialect's word for 'enjoyable'. The milk is heated with peppercorns and saffron, which gives it a striking colour – bright yellow dotted with black, and a fragrant, delicate savoury flavour. It is a semi-hard cheese, with a soft rind, which we serve as part of an *antipasti* selection. As well as its fantastic *mozzarella di bufala* (see page 36), Campania boasts a collection of other creamy cheeses made from mozzarella. *Bocconcini*, meaning 'little mouthfuls', are often served as a starter.

Another interesting Campanian cheese that we often had at home when I was growing up and which I still use a lot, is *provolone del Monaco*. It has been made on the Sorrento peninsula since the eighth century. After the curd paste is shaped into its obligatory pear or cylindrical shape, the cheese is hung for anywhere between 4 and 18 months to produce a semi-hard cheese. The more aged, the spicier and more robust the flavour, at which point it's usually eaten on its own. My father used to have a slice on top of a tomato salad, just with extra virgin olive oil, salt and pepper, which was a perfect balance of sweet and spice.

Puglia is particularly known for its creamy, indulgent cheeses, such as beautiful burrata (see page 23), and its hybrid, *stracciatella*, which means 'torn apart' and is essentially the creamy centre of the burrata – strands of mozzarella swimming in cream. In Puglia, they also mix bocconcini with cream, then serve them with rocket, with crushed walnuts and *mosto cotto* on top, which is decadent yet absolutely delicious. I like to serve mine (without the cream) at room temperature, with crushed pistachios and a little lemon zest on top, then drizzled with honey – for dessert.

PUGLIA IS PARTICULARLY KNOWN FOR ITS CREAMY, INDULGENT CHEESES, SUCH AS BEAUTIFUL BURRATA

Ricotta, again found all over Italy, is perhaps the most versatile cheese as it can be used right the way through your meal. It is also one of the lightest and lowest in fat. Ricotta is made from a by-product of other cheeses – the leftover whey after the curds have been strained to make mozzarella or provolone. The whey is heated – ricotta means 're-cooked' – then strained, and the lumpy cheese produced is *ricotta fresca*. In the South, ricotta is predominantly made from sheep's milk, and while cow's milk ricotta has a very mild flavour and is a good canvas for other flavours, sheep's ricotta is very strong and is best cooked, or heavily sweetened as it is in *cannoli Siciliani* which must only be made from sheep's ricotta.

RICOTTA IS MADE FROM A BY-PRODUCT OF OTHER CHEESES – THE LEFTOVER WHEY AFTER THE CURDS HAVE BEEN STRAINED TO MAKE MOZZARELLA OR PROVOLONE

Sheep's ricotta can also be cured and pressed to become *ricotta salata*, which is semi-hard to hard and has a beautiful strong, salty flavour. We shave it on top of salads or over pasta – any *pasta alla Norma* (see page 71) has to have hard ricotta grated over it before being served.

UOVA AL PURGATORIO

SPICY EGGS

THE TRANSLATION 'EGGS IN PURGATORY' is a strange name for this popular Italian dish, which I think of as something my mum used to make when there was no time to cook. The purgatory refers to the fiery tomato sauce in which you poach the eggs but you can add as much 'fire' as you like. It's so quick and easy to throw this together and although it makes a wonderful breakfast or brunch dish I'd eat it at any time of the day.

SERVES 4

40g n'duja
1 large banana shallot, *finely sliced into rounds*
1 garlic clove, *crushed*
1 Romano pepper, *finely chopped*
10 basil leaves, *plus a few extra leaves to serve*
500ml Tomato Sauce *(see page 272)*
60ml vegetable stock
8 eggs
20g pecorino cheese, *grated*
4 large slices sourdough bread
extra virgin olive oil, *to finish*

Preheat the oven to 220°C / fan 200°C / gas 7.

In a flameproof baking dish set over a medium heat, sweat the n'duja, shallot, garlic and peppers until the shallot is soft and translucent.

Add the basil, tomato sauce and stock and simmer for about 15 minutes.

Crack each egg into the sauce and scatter over half the pecorino. Bake in the oven for 4–5 minutes (depending on how well done you like your eggs) then remove. As the eggs cook, toast the bread and place on four serving plates.

To serve, scoop the eggs out of the sauce and place on top of each bruschetta, then add as much of the sauce as you like. Shave the remaining pecorino over the top of each plate and scatter over a few basil leaves. Serve immediately drizzled with extra virgin olive oil.

ACCIUGHE, PEPERONI E MOZZARELLA DI BUFALA CAMPANA

ANCHOVIES, PEPPERS AND BUFFALO MOZZARELLA

THIS SALAD CAME ABOUT when I was playing with some of my favourite ingredients. It's a simple dish but very complex in terms of its flavours. Anchovies and peppers are both strong flavours. They'd have the potential to fight each other if they were left to their own devices but the gentle acidity of the soft, creamy cheese provides the bridge and creates a perfect fusion of the three.

Although mozzarella made from cow's milk is made all over Italy, as well as in other countries, the production of *mozzarella di bufala* from the Campania region around Naples is tightly regulated and the cheese has been awarded protected status. It has to meet strict criteria governing not just where but how it is produced and it must be made entirely from domestic water buffalo milk to guarantee its unique flavour. The Campania cheese has a more acidic, richer taste than cow's mozzarella and as part of your journey through my collection of southern flavours to try, it's really worth seeking it out. Note that when it's really fresh it should be rubbery.

SERVES 4

4 Romano peppers (about 600g)
70ml extra virgin olive oil, *plus extra to serve*
12 tinned anchovy fillets, *plus 2 tbsp oil from the tin*
4 tsp red wine vinegar (preferably Merlot)
400g mozzarella di bufala Campana (ideally) or another buffalo or cow's mozzarella, *at room temperature, roughly torn*
50g caper berries
1 small Tropea red onion (about 50g) or griotte onion, *thinly sliced and placed in iced water*
handful of basil leaves
sea salt and freshly ground black pepper

On a very hot griddle pan or barbecue, grill the peppers until the skins are blistered and charred. Transfer to a container, cover with cling film and leave to steam and cool.

Meanwhile, make a dressing by whisking together the olive oil, anchovy oil, vinegar and some salt and pepper.

Remove the skin, seed pod and inner ribs from the peppers over a bowl so that you save all the juices. Cut the peppers into wedges and mix them with the dressing and the reserved juices. Season.

Place the peppers in a large serving dish, scatter over the mozzarella, then top with the anchovy fillets, caper berries, drained onion rings and basil. Drizzle with more olive oil if liked.

INSALATA DI MARE

SEAFOOD SALAD

THIS IS A CLASSIC ANTIPASTO FOR SPECIAL OCCASIONS.
In the South we often serve it as a light starter at weddings. Once you've seen
the dish that might seem a bit of a strange choice as it's not really a looker
(I've watched diners poke it with some scepticism), but once you dig your fork
in and taste the harmonious combination of flavours I can guarantee you
won't look back and you'll understand why we consider it pretty exceptional.
If you're serving this to four people it will make quite a large amount, but you
can keep any leftovers in the fridge for up to two days and the flavours will
mature (it possibly tastes even better).

SERVES 4—6

550ml white wine
1 bay leaf
pinch of white peppercorns
2 celery sticks from near the heart, *trimmed and sliced*
2 carrots, *peeled and sliced*
160g squid, *cleaned and cut into 1cm strips*
200g raw Mazara or tiger prawns, *peeled and deveined*
1 garlic clove, *sliced*
1 red chilli, *deseeded and finely chopped*
100ml extra virgin olive oil
500g clams, *cleaned*
500g mussels, *cleaned*
grated zest and juice of ½ lemon
120g cherry tomatoes, *halved*
100g green olives (*I use the Sicilian
    Castelvetrano variety*)
20g flat-leaf parsley, *roughly chopped*
sea salt and freshly ground black pepper

Put 2 litres of water into a large saucepan with 500ml of the wine,
bay leaf, white peppercorns and a pinch of salt and bring to the boil.
Add the celery, carrot, squid and prawns and blanch for 1 minute.
Drain and set aside.

Put the sliced garlic and chilli and 2 tablespoons of the olive oil into
a large, deep saucepan over a medium heat. When the garlic is golden,
add the clams and mussels and the remaining white wine, immediately
cover with a lid and cook on a high heat for about 2—4 minutes,
shaking the pan occasionally, until all the clams and mussels have
opened. Discard any clams and mussels that don't open then remove
the remainder from their shells over a bowl. Keep the liquid but
discard the shells.

Pour 50ml of the reserved shellfish liquid into a deep jug or container,
add 60ml of the olive oil, the lemon zest and juice, some salt and
pepper and blend using a hand blender until you have a smooth and
creamy dressing.

To serve, transfer all the shellfish and blanched vegetables to a serving
dish with the cherry tomatoes, toss with the dressing, the remaining
olive oil and salt and pepper if needed.

Finish by scattering over the olives and the parsley.

CHICULIATA

TUNA TARTARE

MARINATED RAW FISH finds a place in many different cultures' food and this is South Italy's version. We try to bring a mix of different flavours to the marinade – saltiness from the anchovies and olives, sweetness from the tomatoes, a little bit of heat from the chilli and some acidity and freshness from the lemon. And of course, there has to be sunshine in the dish, which we add with our beautiful sun-baked bottarga (for more about this, see page 124). I would usually serve this with the grey mullet bottarga – *bottarga di muggine* – but go for tuna if you prefer.

SERVES 4

400g very fresh tuna, *roughly chopped*
1 tbsp salted capers, *soaked overnight, roughly chopped*
2 tbsp pitted black olives, *roughly chopped*
1 tsp black aniseed or black fennel seeds, *crushed with the flat of a knife*
6–8 tinned anchovy fillets, *rinsed*
3 San Marzano tomatoes, *peeled and cut into small cubes (keep the seeds and juice)*
3 medium-hot green chillies, *cut into very fine strips*
10g chives, *finely chopped*
10g parsley, *finely chopped*
2 tsp extra virgin olive oil, *plus a drizzle to finish*
4 Little Gem lettuce leaves
juice of 1 lemon
1 tbsp bottarga, *finely shaved*
sea salt

In a bowl, mix the tuna, capers, black olives, crushed aniseed and anchovies, then add the tomatoes with their seeds and juice, chillies, chives, parsley and olive oil. Season with salt and mix well.

Pile the mixture into the lettuce leaves and finish by drizzling with olive oil and the lemon juice, then scatter the bottarga over the top.

CRUDO DI BRANZINO

SEA BASS CARPACCIO

'CRUDO' MEANS 'RAW' IN ITALIAN so you could say that this dish is a bit like our version of sashimi. However, unlike the very clean Japanese take, where the fish is the hero, ours is ramped up a little with lemon, salt and lots of extra virgin olive oil – it's as much about the combination of the other ingredients as it is the fish. There are infinite interpretations of the recipe up and down our coastline so this is mine, distinctly southern with its *garum* and Tropea onions, but with the core principles of the dish at its heart. You could use another meaty white fish such as sea bream, gilthead bream or cod in place of the sea bass.

SERVES 4

70ml extra virgin olive oil
1 tbsp lemon juice
1 tsp garum *(anchovy water, see page 123)*
500g sea bass fillet
1 small Tropea red onion or griotte onion
   or 2 spring onions, *finely sliced into rings*
10g flat-leaf parsley leaves
30g radishes
10g chervil
grated zest of ½ lemon
20g salted capers, *soaked overnight*
20g caper berries
sea salt and freshly ground black pepper

In a bowl mix the olive oil, lemon juice and garum with some salt and pepper. Whisk until creamy and set aside.

Slice the sea bass fillet in half, so that you end up with two pieces roughly 5mm thick. Cut each piece in half, then place each between two sheets of cling film and with the flat side of a meat tenderiser or the back of a pan, flatten it down until it's very thin. Gently move each sea bass piece to a separate serving plate and finish by dividing all the other ingredients between each plate, arranging them over the fish. Drizzle over the dressing and serve immediately.

MINESTRA DI LENTICCHIE E PANCETTA

LENTIL SOUP WITH PANCETTA

THIS DISH EVOKES MEMORIES OF MY CHILDHOOD. As kids my brothers and sister and I only wanted to eat pasta and meatballs, but Tuesday night supper was always soup. On Monday night we always ate leftovers from Sundays so there was time for Mum to prepare for Tuesday, which meant soaking her beans for soup the next day. Mum tried really hard to get us to eat pulses. Cannellini and borlotti beans and chickpeas were a real failure, but for some reason we loved lentils. This soup was therefore quite often presented to us on Tuesdays and I still make it for my own children.

Rotonda lentils are my preference here. They are cultivated organically in Basilicata, on the border with Calabria, and are the lentils I grew up with. They range from pinky-brown to beige and give this soup a fabulous colour. Sadly they're not that easy to find in the UK so do substitute Castelluccio or Puy lentils if you're having trouble sourcing them.

SERVES 6 — 8

400g Rotonda, Castelluccio or Puy lentils
1 bay leaf
1 large carrot, *peeled and finely diced*
1 celery stick, *finely diced*
1 large onion, *finely diced*
100g pancetta, *roughly diced*
150ml Tomato Sauce *(see page 272)*
10g chives, *chopped*
10g flat-leaf parsley, *chopped*

Rinse the lentils thoroughly then place in a pot with just enough salted water to cover. Add the bay leaf, carrot, celery, onion, pancetta and tomato sauce, bring to a very gentle simmer and cook for 45 minutes, or until the lentils are tender but still have a slight bite. Add more hot water (not cold) during cooking if necessary to keep the level constantly just above the lentils and always stir lentils with a wooden rather than a metal spoon. Metal cools with the temperature of the water and stops the lentils cooking evenly. Pulses don't like different temperatures!

Remove the pancetta, pat it dry, and fry it in a dry frying pan until crispy, then set aside.

Blend half of the soup. Return the blended soup to the unblended and reheat.

Serve in bowls with the fried pancetta and herbs sprinkled on top.

INSALATA DI BACCALÀ

SALT COD SALAD

THE INSPIRATION FOR THIS RECIPE comes from a dish we often serve at Christmas as part of the main course. The festive version is quite rustic and hearty – pan-fried fish stirred into a rich stew of oily peppers and chunks of potato. This is my lighter, more elegant interpretation, which nods to the original but doesn't have its heaviness. As for my cod marinated in liquorice (see page 120) – the cod is only very lightly cured in the salt.

SERVES 4

1 litre water
150g sea salt
1 bay leaf
5 white peppercorns
3 juniper berries
500g black cod loin or good-quality cod loin
1 tbsp lemon juice
70ml extra virgin olive oil, *plus a little extra for frying*
1 tbsp white wine vinegar
1 tsp clear honey
50g pitted black olives
500g small new potatoes
1 red chilli
80g spring onions
1 thyme sprig
sea salt and freshly ground black pepper

Put the water, salt, bay leaf, peppercorns and juniper berries in a large casserole and bring to the boil. As soon as it starts to boil, take off the heat and leave to cool completely.

When the water is cold, submerge the cod fillet and leave to marinate at room temperature for about 4 hours.

Preheat the oven to 200°C/fan 180°C/gas 6. Whisk the lemon juice, oil, vinegar, honey and some salt and pepper in a bowl, until creamy.

Put the olives into a small baking tray and the potatoes into a roasting tin. Bake the olives for 20 minutes, then remove and leave to cool. Bake the potatoes for about 30 minutes, until soft (it depends how big they are). Remove from the tin and leave to cool at room temperature, then peel and crush them by hand into pieces the size of an almond.

Cut the chilli in half, take out the seeds and cut into very thin strips. Put in iced water for 10 minutes. Slice the white part of the onion and set aside, then cut the green stems into very thin strips and place in the iced water.

When the cod has had its marinating time, preheat the oven to 200°C/fan 180°C/gas 6.

Drain the cod and dry it on kitchen paper. Heat a large non-stick frying pan with a few drops of olive oil and the thyme over a high heat, and fry the cod fillet for 1 minute on each side, until golden. Transfer to a piece of baking paper, fold the paper over the top and finish the cooking in the oven for 6 minutes. Allow to cool a little then flake the flesh. Lay the cod flakes in a serving dish then scatter over the potatoes, olives and onion slices. Pour over the dressing and garnish with the drained chilli curls and green onion strips.

SARDE RIPIENE

STUFFED SARDINES

I PROBABLY SHOULDN'T BE SAYING THIS AS A CHEF but for me sardines can smell and taste a bit strong so cooking them in this way, where a generous stuffing is the real hero, softens the flavour and transforms them. The herbs and lemon zest add freshness and acidity and the gentle background of breadcrumbs and cheese contrasts with the oily fish. This is a classic version of a dish you'll find all over the South. The sardines are butterflied then wrapped around the filling – which varies according to the cook – before they're deep-fried. I've also tucked a basil leaf over and around my filling to help prevent any of it falling out. Sharing these as an *antipasto* always gets people talking, not only as Italians try and work out the cook's choice of ingredients, but because the mozzarella melts and stretches when you bite into them and there's guaranteed to be mess. Serve the sardines with something fresh and crunchy to cut through the richness, such as the fennel, puntarelle, orange and olive salad on page 24 or the caramelised Tropea onion salad on page 179.

SERVES 4

12 medium sardines, *butterflied (ask your fishmonger to remove the backbones but keep them whole with their tails on)*
80g pitted black olives
80g mozzarella
50g sun-dried tomatoes
20g pecorino cheese, *grated*
50g fresh breadcrumbs
½ tsp dried oregano
grated zest of 1 lemon, *plus a little juice*
12 large basil leaves
3 medium eggs
250g dried breadcrumbs
plain flour, to dust
sunflower oil, *for deep-frying*

Wash the sardines. Place the olives, mozzarella and sun-dried tomatoes on a chopping board and chop them all together. Transfer to a bowl and add the pecorino, fresh breadcrumbs, oregano, lemon zest and a few drops of lemon juice. Mix well to get a compact mixture.

Spread some of the mixture down the middle of each sardine. Cover with a basil leaf then roll up the sides of each sardine around the basil leaf so that the leaf tucks the filling inside the fish.

In a bowl, whisk the eggs. Place the dried breadcrumbs on a plate. Dust the sardines with flour, then carefully dip them in the egg one by one and then in the breadcrumbs.

Heat enough oil for deep-frying in a large, deep saucepan or deep fat fryer to 165°C. Fry the sardines in batches for about 3 minutes, remove each batch with a slotted spoon, drain on kitchen paper then deep-fry again for 3 minutes. Drain on kitchen paper again and serve hot.

CALAMARI E CARCIOFI SALTATI

SAUTÉED SQUID WITH ARTICHOKES

THIS IS A FANTASTIC DISH AND VERY EASY TO PREPARE but to ensure you're successful with it there are two instructions to follow carefully. The first is to work quickly when prepping your artichokes and to put the sections straight into the acidulated water so that they don't go brown. The second is to cook your squid fast. Your pan needs to be very, very hot before you put the seafood anywhere near it, and the best way to guarantee perfectly cooked squid is to mix it with the oil before putting it in the pan (rather than putting the oil in the pan), then to sauté it very quickly – just for 30 seconds. The squid will stay beautifully crunchy on the outside but nice and juicy on the inside – a perfect explosion of flavour and texture in your mouth.

SERVES 4

3-4 artichokes, preferably mammole or violet
   (*don't use globe*)
juice of 1 large lemon, *plus the grated zest of ½*
50ml extra virgin olive oil, *plus a little extra for frying*
1 red chilli, *deseeded and finely sliced*
2 mint leaves, *finely sliced*
500g baby squid, *cleaned and cut into 5mm rings*
20g bottarga (mullet roe)
sea salt and freshly ground black pepper

FOR THE PICKLE BRINE

500ml water
500ml muscatel vinegar
1 bay leaf
5 white peppercorns
2 juniper berries

Clean the artichokes by taking off the external leaves until you reach the tender ones. Prepare two bowls of water. Put aside 1 tablespoon of the lemon juice and mix it with the zest, then divide the remaining juice between the bowls of water. Pick the tender artichoke leaves one by one and put into one of the bowls of acidulated water to prevent discolouring. Scoop out the hairy choke with a spoon, slice the artichoke hearts and place in the second bowl. Peel the artichoke stalks, slice them and add to the bowl with the leaves.

Put all the ingredients for the pickle brine into a pan and bring to the boil, then drain the artichoke leaves and sliced stalks and add them to the liquid. Simmer for 2½–3 minutes, until the artichoke is cooked through but still a little crunchy. Drain and place on a kitchen towel to dry and cool.

In a bowl, mix the oil, reserved lemon juice and zest, chilli and mint. Drain the sliced artichoke hearts and leaves, mix with this dressing and set aside.

Heat a frying pan over a high heat, add 1 teaspoon of olive oil and fry the squid and pickled artichokes very quickly, until the squid is golden brown. Check the seasoning and adjust with salt and pepper. Transfer to a serving dish with the artichoke and finish by pouring over the artichoke hearts and dressing and tossing together, then shaving the bottarga over the top.

POMODORO MOSCIAME E PEPERONCINO

TOMATO, MOSCIAME (DRIED TUNA) AND CHILLI SALAD

THIS WAS ONE OF MY FATHER'S FAVOURITE *al fresco* lunches and for me very much reflects the way we eat and cook in the South. He would go to the garden, pick the basil, chillies, tomatoes and onions, run them under cold water, then arrange everything on a plate and finish by grating *mosciame* over the top.

Mosciame is salt-cured tuna loin from Sardinia. In some parts of the island tuna is only fished once a year so drying the expensive loin is a wonderful way of preserving it for leaner times. Methods of curing the tuna vary, but the basic principle is said to have been brought to the island by the Phoenicians and essentially involves salting the tuna for several days then rinsing it and leaving it to dry under the baking Sardinian sun and gentle sea breezes. You can serve mosciame as you would any cured meat, by slicing it, or as my father did, by shaving it into shards and tossing it through a salad. There are different types of mosciame depending on the time they have been left to age; these will range from the slightly moist and chewy to the very dry, so I'd like to encourage you to experiment to find your preference.

SERVES 4

650g mixed seasonal tomatoes *(including cherry tomatoes)*
½ small Tropea red onion, *finely sliced*
80g mosciame (see above), *finely sliced*
10g basil leaves
1 green chilli, *halved, deseeded and roughly chopped*
1 red chilli, *halved, deseeded and roughly chopped*
extra virgin olive oil, *to drizzle*
sea salt

Slice the larger tomatoes into rounds and halve the cherry tomatoes, then place on a plate. Arrange the onion, mosciame, basil and chilli on top. Season with salt and drizzle with extra virgin olive oil, to your taste.

PROVATURA, FAVE E PISELLI

SAUSAGE, BROAD BEANS AND PEAS

AS YOU WILL QUICKLY LEARN IN THIS BOOK, pork is the main meat in the South of Italy and the pig is highly valued and used in every way imaginable; no part of it is wasted. When I was growing up, many families, including my own, used to rear their own pigs so making sausages at home was an everyday task. In my family it was something my grandmother did. These days, although many southerners might buy their sausage meat from a butcher, in Calabria in particular, the tradition of making fresh sausages has lingered. However, before the sausage mix is stuffed into its casings there is the obligatory 'provatura' ritual. 'Provatura' means 'to taste' and at this point the cook will fry off a few pieces of the sausage mixture and place them in the middle of the table for everybody to try. Opinions are thrown out – 'it's too salty', 'too dry', 'needs more chilli', 'more fennel' etc. The idea is that the majority wins and the cook then adds whatever is needed. The sausages are finished and of course everybody claims the credit or complains about what's wrong with them.

SERVES 4

35ml extra virgin olive oil

50g griotte onions or spring onions, *roughly chopped*

120g soft, spicy fresh Calabrian sausage or a very soft cooking chorizo or Tuscan sausage, *skin removed, meat crumbled*

50ml Marsala wine

120g broad beans, *shelled*

120g peas, *shelled*

handful of basil, *roughly chopped*

handful of flat-leaf parsley, *roughly chopped*

handful of mint leaves, *roughly chopped*

30g Sardinian ricotta mustia (available from some Italian delicatessens) or a similar salted, lightly smoked soft cheese or a soft goat's cheese

handful of pea shoots

pinch of black fennel seeds

sea salt and freshly ground black pepper

In a saucepan, heat 4 teaspoons of the olive oil and sweat the onion with a pinch of salt on a low heat until soft. Add the sausage, turn up the heat to high and cook until browned. Add the Marsala and let it evaporate.

In the meantime, blanch the broad beans and peas in salted boiling water for 30 seconds. Drain well and mix with the onion and sausages. Cover the pan with a lid and continue to cook over a medium heat for about 3 minutes until the sausage is cooked through.

Add all the chopped herbs and 1 tablespoon of olive oil and season with salt and pepper.

To serve, arrange the sausage mixture on a heated serving plate. Crumble over the ricotta mustia and top with the pea shoots and a sprinkling of the fennel seeds.

ZUPPE DI CANNELLINI E GAMBERI DI MAZARA

CANNELLINI BEAN SOUP WITH MAZARA PRAWNS

THIS SOUP IS LIKE A LIGHT VERSION OF A CLASSIC
pasta e fagioli (see page 74). It's based on techniques and flavour combinations
I learned from my mum but I've given it a more refined, delicate touch.
Mum would probably throw a huge chunk of pancetta into the cooking broth
thinking my version wasn't hearty enough. This is also great eaten cold, which
might not always be what you want in the midst of a bleak British winter,
but is what I'd most likely choose to do in the 40° heat of a Calabrian summer.

SERVES 4

250g cannellini beans, *soaked in plenty of water overnight*
12 raw Mazara red prawns, *peeled, shells reserved (use tiger prawns if Mazara are unavailable)*
2 carrots
3 celery sticks
85ml extra virgin olive oil
2 shallots, *chopped*
½ tbsp, tomato purée
1 star anise
10 fennel seeds
3 garlic cloves, *sliced*
1 thyme sprig
handful of chervil leaves
sea salt and freshly ground black pepper

Drain the beans and place in a casserole or large saucepan with one of the carrots and one of the celery sticks and pour in just enough cold water to cover.

Bring to the boil and cook gently for about 1 hour, or until tender. If the cooking liquid gets too low during cooking, add more hot water to the pan (don't use cold otherwise you can stop the beans cooking evenly), keeping the water level just above the beans. Remove the vegetables, remove a couple of large spoonfuls of beans and keep on the side with a few spoonfuls of liquid; leave the beans in the pan in their liquid set to one side.

Roughly chop the remaining carrot and celery. Put 2 tablespoons of the olive oil into a shallow sauté pan and sweat the carrot, celery and shallots over a medium heat until soft and the shallots are translucent. Add the prawn shells and toast for a couple of minutes. Add the tomato purée, star anise and fennel seeds, cover with cold water and leave to simmer for 45 minutes uncovered. Pass the liquid through a sieve and into a bowl, then return it to the pan and place over a medium–high heat. Allow it to reduce until creamy and the consistency of a syrup.

Use a hand blender to blend the smaller quantity of reserved beans to a smooth cream. In the meantime, in a pan heat 3 tablespoons of olive oil with the garlic. When the garlic is golden brown, add the thyme and allow to sit in the heat of the oil for a few moments for the flavour to infuse. Pass the oil through a sieve into the creamed beans and blend with a hand blender again.

Drain the liquid from the pan of beans into a jug. Pour about 450ml of liquid – or enough to create your desired consistency of soup – back into the pan then gently reheat until piping hot. Stir through the creamed bean mixture.

Heat the remaining 2 teaspoons of oil in a frying pan over a high heat. Season the prawns with salt and pepper and quickly fry them until lightly coloured and cooked through – about 1 minute.

To serve, divide the soup among heated serving bowls, finishing each with prawns, a scattering of chervil leaves and a drizzle of the prawn syrup.

'IMPEPATA' DI COZZE, VONGOLE, N'DUJA E MARSALA

MUSSELS AND CLAMS IN A PEPPER BROTH WITH N'DUJA AND MARSALA

THE NAME OF THIS SOUP IS A LITTLE MISLEADING: *'impepata'* means 'peppered' yet in fact this recipe has no pepper at all. Like many recipes that evolve, the name now refers to the style of cooking the light broth rather than its principal ingredient. The original dish, which you do still find in some places in Puglia, is quite overpowering – garlic and pepper are both very strong flavours, so the broth here has milder, more fragrant ingredients, such as herbs and fennel seeds, which don't overpower the delicate mussels and clams.

The broth is poured into each dish over thin, crispy, dome-shaped breads called *'puccia'* – 'little cheeks', which once you've made them needs no explanation. *Puccia* are usually stuffed and eaten like sandwiches – they were originally conceived as food for peasants working in the fields as they were easily transportable. Here the bread soaks up all the delicious flavours of the broth and goes soggy, and as with so many frugal southern recipes, they are a canny way of stretching a simple soup so that nobody goes hungry. The dough quantities can easily be doubled so you could make four extra for lunch the next day – pile them high with mozzarella, olives, tomatoes and finish with a drizzle of olive oil.

SERVES 4

1 garlic clove, *smashed with the back of a knife*
5 tbsp extra virgin olive oil
½ small shallot, *chopped*
30g n'duja
50g Basil Sauce *(see page 273)*
500g clams, *cleaned*
500g mussels, *cleaned*
4 tbsp Marsala wine
handful of flat-leaf parsley, *roughly chopped*
handful of chives, *roughly chopped*
1 green chilli, *halved, deseeded and roughly chopped*
½ tsp fennel seeds

Preheat the oven to 220°C / fan 200°C / gas 7.

First make the breads. Make up the dough, following the recipe for pizza dough on page 265.

Divide the dough in half and using a rolling pin flatten each piece to a round shape of about 20cm in diameter. Place on a floured baking tray and bake for 10 minutes, until bubbling. Remove from the oven and lower the oven temperature to 120°C / fan 100°C / gas ½. Slice each bread in half horizontally using a serrated bread knife, then put each disc over a lightly floured upside-down ovenproof bowl, ramekin or baking tin and put back in the oven for about 15 minutes until nice and crispy.

In a large saucepan over a low heat, sweat the garlic in 2 tablespoons of the oil with the shallot until soft but not coloured. Add the n'duja, basil sauce, clams, mussels and Marsala and immediately cover the pan with a lid. Cook on a high heat for about 4–6 minutes, shaking the pan occasionally, until the clams and mussels all open (discard any that don't), then remove from the heat.

FOR THE 'PUCCIA' BREADS

75g strong bread flour, plus a little extra to dust
75g strong '00' flour
1g dried yeast
5g salt
100–125ml water

In the meantime, mix the remaining 3 tablespoons of olive oil with wthe parsley, chives, chilli and fennel seeds.

To serve, place a piece of puccia into the bottom of an individual pasta or soup bowl, pour the mussels and clams and broth over the top and finish each portion with a drizzle of the herb and oil mixture.

BRODO CHINU

BEEF BROTH WITH POACHED EGGS

THIS BROTH IS SOUL FOOD – *mamma's* equivalent of a chicken soup
when you're ill, or something to revive you when you've hit the *vino rosso* a little
too hard the night before… *'Chino'* means full and this broth is indeed stuffed.
Packed with protein, released into the broth from the beef bones and eggs, and
full of vegetables for added vitamins and sustenance. It's rich, hearty, nurturing
and delicious.

SERVES 4

3 spring onions, *trimmed and roughly chopped;
    reserve some of the green part for garnish*
1 celery stick, *diced*
1 carrot, *peeled and cut into rounds*
4 eggs
1 tbsp grated pecorino cheese, *plus extra to serve*
1 tbsp chopped green spring onion

FOR THE BROTH

1kg beef bones
1 large yellow onion, *unpeeled and halved*
3 carrots, *chopped*
3 celery sticks, *chopped*
1 leek, *chopped*
3 juniper berries
2 bay leaves
1 litre dry white wine
8 litres cold water

Preheat the oven to 220°C / fan 200°C / gas 7.

Put the beef bones into a roasting tin and bake for 30 minutes.

Put all the broth ingredients, including the bones, into a large deep
pot, bring to the boil and simmer for 4½ hours. Pour the broth
through a sieve lined with muslin, let the liquid cool and store in the
fridge overnight.

The next day, heat your grill on its highest setting. Scoop the layer
of fat off the top of the broth and heat the liquid on the hob.

Add the onion, celery and carrot and cook for 1 – 2 minutes. Drop
the eggs into the broth, sprinkle with the pecorino and place the pot
under the grill for 2 – 3 minutes (depending on how you like your
egg). To serve, sprinkle with more pecorino and green spring onion.

ZUPPE DI PORCINI, PATATE E CACIOCAVALLO

PORCINI, POTATO AND CACIOCAVALLO SOUP

THERE ARE SEVERAL THEORIES about how the caciocavallo cheese (meaning 'cheese on horseback') got its name but the most likely is that it describes the maturing process and the tradition of tying the cheeses in pairs and hanging them over poles to age, just as they would have been long ago before being thrown over a *'cavallo'*, a donkey's back, to transport them to market. The cheese, which is produced all over southern Italy – though the variety from the Sila mountains has achieved protected status – is made from cow's or sheep's milk and is stretched to give it its characteristic stringy texture (it's from the same family as mozzarella, which has a similar texture). It is then shaped into gourd or teardrop shapes before being tied at the top with string and hung over the poles. It is ripened to various levels of maturity but is essentially quite a firm to hard cheese with a yellow rind and a fruity, earthy, very salty flavour.

The potatoes used here are very floury, so they almost melt when they cook and don't overpower the subtle porcini flavours. The broth is poured over the caciocavallo, causing it to melt, which accentuates its wonderful strings.

SERVES 6

6 tbsp extra virgin olive oil
400g porcini mushrooms (ceps), *wiped, trimmed (reserve the trimmings) and cut into 1cm dice*
1 litre chicken or vegetable stock
1 garlic clove, *sliced*
200g leeks, *cut into matchsticks*
5g rosemary, *very finely chopped*
400g Cyprus or King Edward potatoes, *peeled and cut into 1cm dice*
1 tsp tomato purée
100g caciocavallo cheese (*or cow's mozzarella, not buffalo, if unavailable*)
100g spinach leaves
50g pecorino cheese, *grated, plus extra to serve*
sea salt and freshly ground black pepper

Heat a frying pan with 2 tablespoons of olive oil over a high heat and fry the mushrooms until golden brown, seasoning with salt and pepper. Remove from the pan and set aside.

Put the mushroom trimmings (you should have about 100g) in a saucepan with the stock. Put on a low heat and simmer but never allow the liquid to come to the boil. Leave for 20 minutes then pass through a sieve lined with a tea towel and keep to one side.

Put the garlic into a bowl with 2 tablespoons of the olive oil.

Sweat the leek and rosemary in a saucepan with 2 tablespoons of oil until the rosemary has softened – about 5 minutes. Add the potatoes and stir-fry for a couple of minutes. Pour in enough stock to cover, then add the tomato purée and let the liquid simmer, covered, until the potatoes are halfway cooked, about 8 minutes.

At this point add the sautéed mushrooms, cover again with more stock and cook until the potatoes are soft. Check the seasoning and add salt and pepper as necessary.

To serve, strain the garlic from its oil, reserving the oil (discard the garlic). Place a piece of the caciocavallo in each bowl. Finish the soup by stirring the spinach, pecorino cheese and the garlic oil through it. Pour the soup into the bowls with the caciocavallo and sprinkle each serving with some more grated pecorino.

2
PASTA

STROZZAPRETI CON RICOTTA, BASILICO E PEPERONCINO

STROZZAPRETI WITH RICOTTA, BASIL AND CHILLI

AS NAMES GO, THIS MUST BE UP THERE AMONG THE BEST: *strozzapreti* means 'strangle the priest'. Stories tell that after mass on Sunday, greedy priests used to eat so much of this pasta – too quickly – that they choked and suffocated themselves. Shaping the pasta isn't hard (they're an elongated version of *cavatelli* (see page 79) and are made with an eggless dough, so it's quite hardy to work with, and my tip is to say, use three fingers to roll out each shape; you'll see what I mean.

Ricotta has such a mild flavour that you can use it as a canvas – it fades into the background but can also be pepped up by pairing it with stronger tastes. Here it's the fennel pollen that gives it a lift. I know the pollen is more expensive than buying fennel seeds but a little goes a long way, and the flavour is stronger yet sweeter than the seeds, giving the ricotta a lovely zingy finish, like a mixture of camomile and liquorice.

SERVES 4

500g ricotta
75ml extra virgin olive oil, *plus extra to drizzle*
1 small red chilli, *finely chopped*
8 basil leaves, *torn, plus extra whole leaves to serve*
150ml hot vegetable stock *(or use the pasta cooking liquid)*
1 tsp fennel pollen or crushed fennel seeds
2 tbsp pecorino cheese
sea salt and freshly ground black pepper

FOR THE PASTA DOUGH

500g semola rimacinata flour, *sifted*
250ml warm water
pinch of sea salt

For the pasta dough, put the flour in a bowl. Make a well in the centre and pour in the water then the salt. Using a fork, slowly swirl the flour into the water, beginning with the inner rim of the well, until a dough begins to form. Gather the dough into a mass, work into a ball, then knead for about 10 minutes, until smooth. Let the dough rest, covered with cling film or a clean tea towel, for about 2 hours.

Divide the dough in half, flatten and cut each portion into 2.5cm-wide strips. Using the palms of your hands, roll the dough into 'ropes' roughly 2cm thick, then cut the ropes into 5cm lengths. Lightly dust with flour and place on a floured tray, covered with a tea towel, while you repeat this process with the remaining dough.

To shape the strozzapreti, lay a piece of dough on the surface and pull the dough toward you with three fingers using medium pressure. It should roll as you pull. The first few might be difficult and may not be beautiful, but don't worry – shaping gets easier as you develop a feel for the dough.

continued overleaf

Drop the pasta into a pan of salted boiling water and as soon as they float, drain them, reserving the water, if you're using it for the sauce. Mix the ricotta, olive oil, chilli, basil leaves and stock (or pasta water) and season, then stir the sauce into the pasta.

Transfer to a heated serving dish, sprinkle with the fennel pollen or crushed seeds, drizzle over some olive oil, then add the pecorino and garnish with a couple of basil leaves.

ZITONI ALLA NORMA

PASTA WITH AUBERGINES AND TOMATOES

'ZITI' MEANS 'FIANCÉ' so it's probably no surprise that this type of pasta is one of the main dishes served at weddings. *Ziti* are long, thin rectangular tubes, and *zitoni (or penne candela* as they're also called) are their big brother – wider and more versatile as they're big enough to be stuffed, or as the Sicilians do, made into pies or savoury pasta 'cakes'. *Pasta alla Norma* is one of Sicily's most famous recipes, made with several of the island's sun-soaked riches – aubergine, tomato and basil. Supposedly the dish was named in the nineteenth century, when theatre director and writer Nino Martoglio tasted the sauce and was so impressed by it that he compared it to Vincenzo Bellini's opera masterpiece, *Norma*. The reasons I return to this dish time and again are simple: my wife is Sicilian and my children love slurping *zitoni* so it keeps everybody happy. You need to buy dried pasta for this recipe, never fresh.

SERVES 4

2 tbsp olive oil
1 garlic clove, *sliced*
8 basil leaves, *plus a few extra to garnish*
10 tinned anchovy fillets, *drained*
1 tbsp capers
250ml Tomato Sauce *(see page 272)*
400g zitoni (or candele lunghe snapped in half)
about 500ml sunflower oil
1 aubergine, *halved lenghtways,each half cut into 6 slices*
plain flour, *to dust*
2 tbsp pecorino cheese
2 tbsp aged ricotta shavings

Place the oil in a saucepan over a medium heat and sweat the garlic until golden. Add the basil, anchovies, capers and tomato sauce and heat through, then keep on a low heat.

Cook the zitoni according to the packet instructions, until al dente, then drain, reserving 250ml of the cooking liquid.

While the pasta is cooking, heat the sunflower oil in a deep saucepan or fat fryer until it reaches 185°C. Dust the aubergine slices with flour and fry the aubergines until nice and golden. Remove and drain on kitchen paper. It is important to coat the aubergines in the flour as this stops the oil getting to the flesh and prevents the aubergines going soggy.

Stir the pasta into the sauce with about a ladleful of the reserved cooking liquid. Mix well, add the pecorino, then divide between warmed serving bowls, top with the fried aubergine slices, then sprinkle over the ricotta and extra basil leaves.

ORECHIETTE E CIME DI RAPA

ORECHIETTE WITH TURNIP TOPS

ALONG WITH CAVATELLI (see page 79), *orechiette* are the other principal pasta to come from Puglia, and the 'little ears' are still prepared fresh daily in most homes. They are most commonly made with *semola di grano duro* or *semola rimacinata* as per the recipe here, but also sometimes with *grano arso* (burnt flour). *Grano arso* is now one of the most expensive flours to come by, which is ironic, because like so many southern foods, its origins are humble. In former times, when the wheat was harvested, landowners would burn the stumps left in the fields. These were swept up by the poor and ground at mills into what was basically burnt flour. These days, *grano arso* is made using a simpler toasting process but it has retained its wonderful smokey, nutty flavour. If you are able to source it, do try substituting 100g of the *semola rimacinata* for *grano arso*.

SERVES 4

500g cime di rapa (turnip tops)
1 garlic clove, *thinly sliced*
1 red chilli, *thinly sliced*
2 tbsp extra virgin olive oil, *plus extra to serve*
50g pecorino cheese, *grated*
sea salt

FOR THE PASTA DOUGH

500g semola rimacinata flour, *sifted*
250ml warm water
pinch of salt

For the pasta dough, put the flour in a bowl, make a well in the centre and pour in the water then the salt. Using a fork, slowly swirl the flour into the water, beginning with the inner rim of the well, until a dough begins to form. Gather the dough into a mass, work into a ball, then knead for about 10 minutes, until smooth. Let the dough rest, covered with cling film or a clean tea towel, for 1–2 hours.

Put the turnip tops into a large bowl and cover with iced water. Set aside for about 30 minutes.

Divide the dough into four pieces. On a lightly floured work surface, use the palms of your hands to roll the dough into 'ropes', roughly 1.5cm thick, then cut the ropes into 5mm–1cm pieces. Shape each piece into a round again, then press each piece down in the centre with a knife to make a little ear shape. You can also do this with your thumb or finger. Lightly dust with flour and place on a floured tray, covered with a tea towel, while you repeat this process with the remaining dough.

Cook the turnip tops in boiling salted water for about 10 minutes. Then put the orechiette in the same pot and as soon as they float, cook for a further 2–3 minutes.

Meanwhile, put the garlic and chilli into a pan with the olive oil and fry over a medium heat until the garlic is golden brown. Drain the orechiette and turnip tops, reserving the cooking water.

Add the pasta and turnip tops to the pan of garlic with 100ml of the reserved cooking liquid. Stir then leave for a few minutes, for the garlicky oil to flavour the pasta and vegetables, then transfer to a heated serving dish and finish with a drizzle of olive oil and the pecorino cheese sprinkled over the top.

PASTA FAGIOLI E COZZE

PASTA WITH BEANS AND MUSSELS

THE CHANCES ARE, IF YOU'VE BEEN TO ITALY, you've tried a version of this hearty thick soup, as there are as many variations as regions, provinces, cooks and ingredients. But while you will encounter *pasta fagioli* all over Italy, more than likely, you'll only find it served with mussels in Naples. Both economical and filling, the dish hails from the *cucina povera* style of cooking and it is its thick, creamy consistency that makes it so unique. By cooking the pasta in the 'soup' – the bean and vegetable base – you ensure that all its starchiness is retained and thickens the soup. Combined with the creamy beans, it is an incredibly comforting, rib-sticking dish. For an authentic *pasta fagioli e cozze*, it is important to add the liquid the mussels are cooked in for the fishy flavour they add.

SERVES 4 AS A MAIN COURSE, 6 AS A STARTER

100g cannellini or borlotti beans, *soaked overnight in plenty of cold water*
½ celery stick, *finely chopped*
½ small carrot, *peeled and finely chopped*
½ banana shallot, *finely chopped*
1 bay leaf
1 tbsp extra virgin olive oil
¼ garlic clove, *finely sliced*
¼ red chilli, *deseeded and finely sliced*
250g mussels, *cleaned*
2 tbsp white wine
50g dried tubettini
15g flat-leaf parsley, *roughly chopped*
sea salt and freshly ground black pepper

Drain the beans, wash them with cold water and place in a casserole. Add the vegetables and bay leaf and pour in enough water just to cover (do not add salt). Bring to the boil then lower the heat and simmer for 1 – 1½ hours until they are really soft, leaving the lid half on. Keep checking the level of the liquid and top up with more boiling water if necessary. Turn off the heat and leave the beans in their liquid.

In a deep saucepan heat the oil with the garlic and chilli over a medium heat and when the garlic is golden add the mussels and the wine. Immediately cover with a lid and cook on a high heat for about 2 – 4 minutes, shaking the pan occasionally, until all the mussels have opened (discard any that haven't), then remove from the heat. Remove the mussels from their shells and put in a bowl. Strain the cooking liquid through a fine sieve into a bowl and reserve.

Using a slotted spoon, remove a third of the cooked beans and place them in a bowl with the reserved mussel cooking liquid. Blend to a smooth cream. Return the creamed beans to the pan and bring to the boil. Check the seasoning and adjust accordingly.

Meanwhile cook the pasta in salted boiling water for half the time suggested on the packet, drain it and add to the pot of boiling beans for the second half of the cooking time. When the pasta is cooked to your liking, remove from the heat, add the mussels, check the seasoning and transfer to a warm serving dish. Finish by scattering over the parsley and serve immediately.

LINGUINE CON GAMBERETTI, LIMONE E PREZZOMOLO

LINGUINE WITH PRAWNS, LEMON AND PARSLEY

IF THERE WERE ANY NEED to prove to you how simple southern Italian cooking is, this dish is it. To me, it says 'summer on a plate'. Serve it *al fresco*: stick the pot in the middle of the table and let everyone dive in. A crisp glass of Vermentino rounds off the picture perfectly.

SERVES 4

320g dried linguine
1 garlic clove, *thinly sliced*
1 red chilli, *thinly sliced*
3 tbsp extra virgin olive oil
500g raw tiger prawns, *peeled and roughly chopped*
grated zest of ½ lemon
50g flat-leaf parsley, *roughly chopped*

Bring a pan of salted water to the boil, add the linguine and cook for 3 minutes less than advised on the packet.

Put the garlic and chilli into a saucepan with 2 tablespoons of the olive oil and fry until the garlic is golden brown.

Pour 100ml of water from the linguine pan into the pan of garlic. Drain the linguine, then add it to the pan of garlic and cook the linguine for the final 3 minutes of its cooking time.

When there are just 30 seconds of the cooking time left add the prawns and quickly stir them through, then take the pan off the heat and add the lemon zest, parsley and remaining tablespoon of olive oil until you have a creamy sauce. The heat from the pan will cook the prawns in seconds. Transfer to a heated serving dish and serve immediately.

CAVATELLI N'DUJA, POMODORO E RICOTTA DURA

CAVATELLI WITH N'DUJA, TOMATOES AND AGED RICOTTA

IF THERE'S ONE THING I AM VERY PROUD OF, it's having helped to start a food trend in the UK. Until recently, the Calabrian spiced pork paste, *n'duja*, was practically unknown in this country but once I put it on the menus I created for Pizza Express, news of its rich, porky flavour and fiery heat spread and it has been hailed as an extraordinary Italian discovery. For more about *n'duja* and other Calabrian *salumi* see page 147.

Cavatelli is another Puglian pasta but you will find it all over South Italy, and like the majority of fresh pasta dough recipes from the South, it is eggless, so it is economical but also easier to work with than the softer, stretchier egg doughs.

SERVES 4

60g n'duja
250ml Tomato Sauce *(see page 272)*
50g aged ricotta
2 tsp extra virgin olive oil
basil leaves

FOR THE PASTA DOUGH

400g semola rimacinata flour, *sifted*
220ml warm water
pinch of sea salt

For the pasta dough, put the flour in a bowl. Make a well in the centre and pour in the water then the salt. Using a fork, slowly swirl the flour into the water, beginning with the inner rim of the well, until a dough begins to form. Gather the dough into a mass, work into a ball, then knead for about 10 minutes, until smooth. Let the dough rest, covered with cling film or a clean tea towel, for 2 hours.

Divide the dough in half, flatten and cut the portions into 2.5cm-wide strips. Using the palms of your hands, roll the dough into 'ropes' roughly 1.5cm thick. Lay these ropes on a lightly floured work surface and roll out to 0.5cm in diameter. Cut the rope of dough into 1.5cm lengths. Lightly dust with flour and place on a floured tray, covered with a tea towel, while you repeat this process with the remaining dough.

To shape the cavatelli, lay a piece of dough on the surface and pull the dough toward you with two fingers using medium pressure. It should roll as you pull. The first few might be difficult and may not be beautiful, but don't worry – shaping gets easier as you develop a feel for the dough. To stop the pasta going hard and enable you to keep it for longer I always blanch the cavatelli at this stage. Drop them into a pan of salted boiling water and as soon as they float lift them out with a slotted spoon. Mix them with a little olive oil so they don't stick then put them into sealable packets in the fridge, if using shortly, or the freezer if you want to keep them.

continued overleaf

When ready to serve, blanch the cavatelli in salted, boiling water until they float (you can also cook them straight from frozen), then drain, reserving a ladleful or two of the cooking water.

For the sauce, fry the n'duja in a pan set over a medium heat just until it melts. Add the tomato sauce, then two-thirds of the ricotta and mix well.

Toss the pasta with the sauce, adding a little of the reserved pasta water to loosen it. Spoon into heated serving dishes and serve with the remaining ricotta grated on top, the olive oil drizzled over and some fresh basil leaves.

FILEI CON RAGÙ DI CASTRATO

A RAGÙ, OR AS IT IS ALSO KNOWN, A SUGO, is a meat-based sauce served with pasta. There are thousands of different versions but the most famous outside Italy is undoubtedly the *ragù alla bolognese* – which needs no explanation I'm sure. The *bolognese* characterises the style found in the North – minced meat is cooked in a liquid, such as stock, wine or tomatoes, and simmered with vegetables. In the South a *ragù* is a different proposition, but it is just as deeply rooted in our cuisine, particularly in the Campania region. The *ragù alla napoletana* with its pulpy, rich sauce made from beautiful San Marzano tomatoes is very often what Neapolitan families eat for lunch on Sundays. Neapolitans simmer whole cuts of meat slowly in the sauce. After several hours, the meat will be lifted out of the pot and either served alongside the pasta, which is tossed in the thick *ragù*, or more commonly as a separate course entirely. In Calabria, *ragùs* are more like stews – we simmer chunks of meat in a tomato base as I have here. Each to their own.

Filei is a fantastic Calabrian pasta made by shaping lengths of dough around iron sticks called *ferretto* – they're a bit like long macaroni. The hollow shape, with its irregular surface, is perfect for holding loads of juice from the sauce, and the stretched dough absorbs it as well, so it's saturated with the flavour.

SERVES 4

2 tbsp olive oil
300g boneless lamb shoulder, *cut into 3cm cubes*
1 small spring carrot, *peeled and finely chopped*
1 celery stick, *finely chopped*
1 banana shallot, *finely chopped*
1 tbsp diced unsmoked pancetta
65ml white wine
1 tbsp tomato purée
375ml chicken stock
2 tbsp grated pecorino

FOR THE PASTA DOUGH
250g semola rimacinata flour, *sifted*
130ml warm water
pinch of sea salt

For the pasta dough, put the flour in a bowl. Make a well in the centre and pour in the water then the salt. Using a fork, slowly swirl the flour into the water, beginning with the inner rim of the well, until a dough begins to form. Gather the dough into a mass, work into a ball, then knead for about 10 minutes, until smooth. Let the dough rest, covered with cling film or a clean tea towel, for 1 – 2 hours, while you cook the lamb.

Heat 1 tablespoon of the oil in a large frying pan over a medium heat, and fry the lamb pieces, in batches, until browned. Transfer to a colander to drain the fat.

In a saucepan over a medium heat, sweat the vegetables in the remaining tablespoon of olive oil with the pancetta until softened but not coloured. Add the wine and lamb to the vegetables and cook until the liquid has reduced by half.

continues overleaf

Add the tomato purée and stock and simmer for 2 hours, covered with a lid, stirring occasionally, until you have a rich sauce. If the liquid evaporates completely, stir in another 100ml or so of boiling water.

Divide the pasta dough in half, flatten and roll out using a pasta machine or a rolling pin on a lightly floured surface until 1mm thick. Cut into 1cm-wide strips around 10cm long. Lay a piece of dough along the length of a thick wooden skewer or knitting needle. Press the skewer down a little and turn it around. Squeeze the pasta together along its length to seal it. Roll it out on the work surface and remove the skewer. (Don't expect each one to be perfect - it doesn't matter.)

Place the filei in salted boiling water and when it floats cook for a further 3–4 minutes. Drain and mix into the lamb sauce. Sprinkle with the pecorino to serve.

CITRUS FRUITS

Clockwise from top left: Sanguinello, cedro, sfusato Amalfitano (Amalfi lemons), clementine, Tarocco orange, halved bergamot, whole bergamot, halved cedro.

THE DARK LEAVES AND BRIGHT FRUITS of Italy's citrus trees saturate the landscape the length of the country, but it is the fruits from the South, grown in sun-soaked soil and warmed by gentle sea breezes, that have a unique balance of flavour and, of course, play an integral role in southern Italian cooking.

My home region, Calabria, is particularly renowned for its *bergamotto* (bergamot). The fruit grown along this stretch of coastline is thought to be the best in the world and is the most sought after, due to the fertile soils and warm *ponentino* wind that blows into the region from the Mediterranean.

Known abroad for the citrus notes it lends Earl Grey tea, bergamot is a yellow–orange fruit, similar to a mandarin. The pale rosy flesh is extremely sour, but it has a subtle, floral undertone, which you don't find in any of its relations in the citrus family. The fine, smooth rind releases an aromatic oil, and is the part used to flavour the tea, but it is also an important component in the perfume industry, highly valued for its fragrance but also for its fixing qualities.

From the end of October to the beginning of December – the best time for harvesting them – Calabrian producers harvest three varieties of bergamot: the Fantastico, Castagnaro and Femminello. The latter is widely considered the best and the most versatile but it is also the hardest to find.

Citrus fruits are widely acknowledged as being good for us due to their antioxidants and high levels of vitamin C, but for years my doctor at home has been telling me that I should drink a glass of bergamot juice every day throughout its season claiming it is good for cholesterol and cardiovascular health. It turns out he was right. A few years ago medical researchers announced that bergamot's high proportion of citrus polyphenols, which is also what gives

THE PALE ROSY FLESH IS EXTREMELY SOUR, BUT IT HAS A SUBTLE, FLORAL UNDERTONE

it its bitterness, may be helpful in reducing bad, and raising good cholesterol and lowering blood sugars.

Bergamot hadn't really been used in cooking in this country until a few years ago, but it has stealthily crept into chefs' and home cooks' repertoires and many now make it their citrus fruit of choice. You need to be careful how you use it though, as the flavour can be very overpowering – like a perfume. In my own cooking I am most likely to use the rind rather than the juice as the flavour it imparts is milder and less acidic. I pare or grate the zest for marinades for game, hare and venison (see page 172), but if balanced with sugar in a sorbet, the sharp juice does make for a wonderful palate cleanser.

Seafood will also stand up to the juice's floral potency; cuttlefish is a particularly good match (see page 129). For something a little different, twist a piece of bergamot zest into a glass of hot brandy – it's wonderfully Christmassy and the flavour is fantastic.

Cedro (citron fruit) are perhaps an even lesser known member of the citrus family, which is a shame, because they are wonderful – fragrant and sweet. They look like huge lumpy limes or lemons (the colour depends on their maturity), with wrinkled peel, and indeed their skin is what they are most prized for as it is very thick and tender; they have very little fruit. Sadly they are quite difficult to come by in the UK and you are most likely to find them candied, which is how they are used in southern Italy and Sicily, above all in the famous Sicilan dessert *Cassata* (see page 230).

BERGAMOT HADN'T REALLY BEEN USED IN COOKING IN THIS COUNTRY UNTIL A FEW YEARS AGO

Arancia rossa (blood oranges) arrive in the UK just before Christmas, bringing a welcome splash of colour and sunshine to dark winter days. I look forward to their arrival every year and to savouring my obligatory Campari and blood orange soda. Their juice is more acidic than ordinary oranges and although we tend to think of them as ruby red, the colour of their flesh ranges from pale rose, like a pink grapefruit, to deep, dark crimson.

The colour depends on the variety: Moro are the sweetest and have the darkest colour – they can sometimes be almost black; while Sanguinello oranges are paler in colour, slightly sharper and have a longer growing season. Although they are cultivated across Italy, Sicilian blood oranges are considered the most flavoursome. Grown on the slopes of Mount Etna, they thrive in the fertile, volcanic soil and the unusual climate conditions – warm days and cool nights.

SICILIAN BLOOD ORANGES ARE CONSIDERED THE MOST FLAVOURSOME

Like all citrus fruits they are extremely versatile and while they are interchangeable with normal oranges in recipes, there is something unique about the flavour combination of their bitter 'kick' and their sweetness, which makes them special. I cannot stress enough why you should try them with burrata (see page 23). The contrast of the salty, creamy cheese and gentle bite of the blood orange's faint sharpness is simply fantastic and I would travel far to find the best burrata for serving with the ruby treasures. But sorbets, jams and drinks are all happy vehicles for this wonderful fruit.

LINGUINE AGLIO, OLIO E BOTTARGA

LINGUINE WITH GARLIC, OIL AND BOTTARGA

'AGLIO E OLIO' is the simplest version of this national staple, a pure celebration of pasta in which *spaghetti* or *linguine* are tossed with nothing more than garlic and oil. Chilli is another popular addition, particularly in the South, but this version, with bottarga, too, is my favourite. The dried mullet roe refines the dish a little and gives the sauce a creaminess without adding lots of extra fat. That said, sometimes the simplest dishes are the hardest to get right and this is one that causes a lot of disagreements among chefs and cooks. Each has their perfect ratio of ingredients, which has most likely been refined over years to suit their tastes, and so we all have strong views on how we like it. It's slightly shameful to admit that sometimes we compete over whose is best.

SERVES 4

2 garlic cloves, *thinly sliced*
2 red chillies, *thinly sliced*
3 tbsp extra virgin olive oil
320g dried linguine
80g bottarga (dried mullet roe), *grated*
½ bunch flat-leaf parsley, *chopped*
sea salt

Put the garlic and chillies into a saucepan with 2 tablespoons of the olive oil over a medium heat and fry until the garlic is golden brown.

Bring a pan of salted water to the boil, add the linguine and cook for 3 minutes less than advised on the packet. Stir 100ml of water from the linguine pan into the pan of garlic.

Drain the linguine, then add it to the garlic for the final 3 minutes of the cooking time. Add some more of the pasta water if needed, to make sure the pasta is cooked to your liking. Add half the bottarga and toss it through, then add the parsley and the final tablespoon of olive oil and stir to get a creamy sauce.

Transfer to a heated serving dish and sprinkle the rest of the bottarga over the top.

GNOCCHI DI PATATA CON BACCALÀ E STRASCINATO

POTATO GNOCCHI WITH COD AND PAPRIKA BREADCRUMBS

THERE'S A STRONG TRADITION OF BREAD-MAKING in my region, particularly in my home town, Cerchiara, whose bread (named after the town) is widely considered one of the best in Italy (see page 256). For many families, bread is at the heart of a meal and family life – it nourishes and sustains, but it has also provided livelihoods for the many bakers you will still find in the South. So it follows that there will always be breadcrumbs and where I come from they are considered the 'cheese of the poor'. During lean times, when there wasn't much to eat, breadcrumbs were a canny way of adding flavour, texture and bulk to meals and you will find them featuring in many old recipes from Puglia, Calabria and Basilicata. '*Strascinato*' is the word used for the breadcrumbs in this dish, literally meaning 'dragged' because they are dragged through paprika and oil. Dried out in the oven until crisp and extremely crunchy, they provide a wonderful, flavoursome contrast to the very soft gnocchi and fish.

SERVES 4

FOR THE COD

200g cod fillet, *cut into 1.5cm cubes*
100g coarse salt
200ml milk
about 500ml sunflower oil, *for deep-frying*
100g plain flour

FOR THE BREADCRUMBS

75g fresh breadcrumbs (*ideally from a coarse bread, such as ciabatta*)
3 tbsp extra virgin olive oil
½ garlic clove, *crushed with the back of a knife*
6–8 anchovy fillets
½ red chilli, *sliced*
1 tbsp sweet paprika

Start by preparing the cod. Place the fish in a tray, cover with the salt and leave to marinate for 3 hours.

Preheat the oven to 100°C / fan 80°C / gas ¼. Place the breadcrumbs on a baking tray in the oven and leave for 30 minutes, until dry and hard. Remove and leave to cool, then use your hands or a food processor to crush into fine crumbs.

In a saucepan, heat the oil with the garlic, anchovies and chilli over a medium heat. Cook gently until the garlic is golden brown and the anchovies are melted, then remove from the heat, add the paprika and mix well. Pass the mixture through a sieve and pour over the breadcrumbs. Return to the oven for about 20 minutes or until dry.

continued overleaf

SEMOLA

DURUM WHEAT

LIKE SO MANY THINGS CONCERNING FOOD, while pasta's importance to our cuisine is something Italians all agree on, it is still a subject we can argue about very passionately. Fresh, dried, shape, size, type of sauce – the debates could happily keep us occupied for hours.

The big distinction is, of course, regional. In keeping with the *cucina povera* tradition, the pasta you find in the South is more rustic and frugally inspired, and both fresh and dried pastas are traditionally made from a simple eggless dough, using a much coarser type of flour than in the North.

The hot southern climate is perfect for growing durum wheat, which is a hard, strong, protein-rich wheat. The wheat is milled to make *semola di grano duro*, then 're-ground' to make a slightly smoother flour – *farina di semola rimacinata*. Some pasta in the South is made from the *semola di grano duro* alone but this type of dough is very firm and quite hard to work with, so for all the pasta recipes in this book I've used *semola rimacinata* (with the exception of one egg-based pasta dough, see page 96, which uses 'oo' flour). It's not difficult to come by and I've given you a list of stockists on page 286.

The northern provinces specialise in fresh pasta and the doughs are silky and rich, made with eggs. They also traditionally use a softer wheat, and the very finely milled 'oo' grade of the resulting flour, which is refined and smooth and produces a soft, stretchy dough. Eggs are added to give the dough strength and bite, but this type of pasta remains best suited to being cut into shapes or lengths, such as *tagliatelle* or *fettuccine*, or wrapped around fillings – as *ravioli* and *tortellini*.

The *semola* doughs, made from just the flour and water, are stiff. They are designed to withstand the strength of the presses, which mould them into dry pasta shapes, or be malleable in the hands that shape the fresh pasta, as is still the tradition for many southern types of fresh pasta. Pasta made from a *semola rimacinata* flour also has a grainy, rough surface, which makes it perfect for absorbing its sauce, and for me, good pasta should always taste of its sauce.

In Italy there is no division between the quality of fresh and dried pasta; neither is considered superior, each simply has different uses and suits different types of sauce, and any distinction comes from the raw materials. Certain regions in the *mezzogiorno* – Abruzzo, Molise and Campania, for example – will argue

THE HOT SOUTHERN CLIMATE IS PERFECT FOR GROWING SEMOLA, WHICH IS A HARD, STRONG, PROTEIN-RICH WHEAT

that the quality of the water greatly affects the flavour of the finished product. The Abruzzese brand of dried pasta, De Cecco, and Molise's La Molisana brand are both proud to use mountain spring water, and in the case of De Cecco, they own the source of the spring, which is right next to its factory. And unlike many products we buy today, the commercial brands of dried pasta are respected and trusted and these are the ones you will most likely find in an Italian's home.

LAGANE CECI E COTICHE

FRESH PASTA WITH PORK SKIN AND CHICKPEA

A CROSS BETWEEN A SOUP AND A STEW, this dish is the one I prepared for my first cookery competition when I was 16. I remember soaking the chickpeas in my bedroom the night before I travelled up to Liguria and was so disappointed when I came second. The judges felt that the dish was too rustic (plus I made the error of forgetting to bring a wine match, which we had been asked to do). I suppose in some ways they were right because this is South Italian peasant food at its heartiest. *Lagane* are short, wide, eggless pasta ribbons, traditionally made from *semola di grano duro*, which is one of the least refined durum wheat flours (see page 93) so it has a coarse texture and means the pasta is quite chewy. I've used *semola rimacinata*, which is a slightly finer version of it and is easier to come by in the UK.

Cooking the pork belly slowly in the broth keeps the meat moist and gives it a meltingly soft texture but it means it's definitely a dish for pork lovers as the flavour that permeates the rest of the dish is very strong. If you're not as much of a fan as we are in South Italy, you can leave it out and serve this as a vegetarian dish instead.

SERVES 8

FOR THE PORK SKIN
200g pork skin, from the belly, *in a single piece*
50g pancetta
1 rosemary sprig
20g flat-leaf parsley
¼ garlic clove
5g black peppercorns, *crushed in a mortar
    or spice grinder*

FOR THE CHICKPEAS
300g chickpeas, *soaked overnight in cold water*
1 carrot, *cut into 5mm dice*
1 celery stick, *cut into 5mm dice*
½ medium onion, *cut into 5mm dice*
3 tbsp extra virgin olive oil
1 garlic clove, *smashed with the back of a knife*
1 thyme sprig
2 tsp sweet paprika
sea salt

For the pork, carefully remove the fat from the skin, then with the long side facing you, cut the skin crossways into four pieces.

Place the pancetta, rosemary, parsley and garlic in a food processor and process until you have a paste. Mix everything very well then mix with the crushed black pepper. Spread the mixture over the inside of the pieces of pork skin, then roll each piece up very tightly, so each roll is as thin as you can make it, and secure with kitchen string.

Drain the chickpeas and place in a pot with the pork rolls, carrot, celery and onion and pour in just enough cold water to cover. Bring to a boil and simmer for 1–2 hours, until the chickpeas are tender but still have a slight bite, then add salt to taste, and cook for a few minutes more. If the cooking liquid gets too low during cooking, add more hot water to the pan (don't use cold water otherwise you can stop the chickpeas cooking evenly), keeping the water level just above the chickpeas. Using a slotted spoon, remove the pork rolls and half the chickpeas and keep on the side. Using a hand blender, blend the remaining chickpeas and their liquid until smooth.

FOR THE PASTA DOUGH
250g semola rimacinata flour, *sifted*
130ml warm water
pinch of sea salt

TO FINISH
flat-leaf parsley, *roughly chopped*
extra virgin olive oil

In a saucepan, heat the olive oil with the garlic and thyme over a medium heat. When the garlic is golden brown, remove from the heat and add the paprika. Pass through a sieve and add to the blended chickpeas along with the reserved chickpeas and pork rolls.

For the pasta dough, put the flour in a bowl. Make a well in the centre and pour in the water then the salt. Using a fork, slowly swirl the flour into the water, beginning with the inner rim of the well, until a dough begins to form. Gather the dough into a mass, work into a ball, then knead for about 10 minutes, until smooth. Let the dough rest, covered with cling film or a clean tea towel, for 1–2 hours.

On a lightly floured surface, roll the dough out using a pasta machine or a rolling pin until it's 1mm thick, then cut into strips of 10 × 0.5cm.

Bring a pan of salted water to the boil, and at the same time, gently bring the chickpea mixture to the boil.

Blanch the pasta in the water for 1 minute, then drain and add them to the pan of boiling chickpeas and cook for 2–3 minutes.

Divide the soup among heated serving bowls, topping each portion with a pork roll, and finish with the chopped parsley and a drizzle of olive oil.

PASTA CHIJNA

STUFFED PASTA

I WRESTLED WITH MYSELF OVER WHETHER to put this recipe in the book as I've got to be honest, it's going to take you a bit of time to make and if you embark on it, which I really hope you do – you need to think of it as a labour of love, a lasagne of riches. That said, it's a dish that keeps on giving and it will happily sit in your fridge for 4–5 days so that you'll have lunches and easy meals for a few days afterwards. I felt it was just too good to be missed.

Even at home this is something for weekend cooking or for special occasions and traditionally something mums used to make before their children went away to university or off to the army. I think it's even better the second or third day when it firms up and you can cut a stiff slice and eat it cold. Mum used to dip it in a mixture of beaten egg, basil and pecorino cheese and pan-fry it so that it became like a hot sandwich; we used to take them to the beach.

SERVES 10

FOR THE EGG PASTA DOUGH
90g '00' flour
90g hard durum wheat flour
2 medium eggs

FOR THE EGG AND NETTLE PASTA DOUGH
50g raw nettles, *leaves only (or use 50g spinach)*
2g fresh oregano *(if using spinach instead of nettle)*
5g parsley *(if using spinach instead of nettle)*
1 medium egg
70g '00' flour
70g of hard durum wheat flour

Make the plain egg pasta dough. Mix the '00' flour and durum wheat flour together in a bowl, before adding the eggs. Mix gently to form a dough, adding a little water if necessary. Transfer to a lightly floured work surface and knead the dough until smooth. Wrap in cling film and leave to rest in the fridge for at least 1 hour.

For the nettle pasta dough, wash the nettles or spinach and transfer the wet leaves to a pan with 1–2 tablespoons of water. Cover with a lid and cook over a medium heat for a few minutes, until wilted. Drain and squeeze out any excess water. Purée the nettles (or the spinach together with the oregano and parsley) until smooth – you may need to add some of the egg to help smooth it out. Mix with the '00' flour, durum wheat flour and add the egg or remaining egg, as you did with the plain dough. Place the dough on a lightly floured work surface and knead until smooth. Wrap in cling film and leave to rest in the fridge for at least 1 hour.

Using a pasta machine, roll out both the plain and nettle pasta doughs using setting 5 on your machine (until 1mm thick), then cut into long sheets. Blanch in salted boiling water for approximately 40 seconds. Remove using a large slotted spoon, cool the sheets in iced water, then strain and dry on a clean tea towel. Store in the fridge between layers of cling film until required.

continued overleaf

FOR THE BÉCHAMEL SAUCE
550ml milk
freshly grated nutmeg
35g unsalted butter
40g plain flour
sea salt and freshly ground pepper

FOR THE MEAT STRIPS
100g rustic-style bread, *such as ciabatta*
125ml milk
10g flat-leaf parsley, *roughly chopped*
½ garlic clove, *crushed*
75g minced beef
75g minced veal
25g Grana Padano cheese, *grated*
2 tsp sweet paprika

**FOR THE SPINACH AND RICOTTA
STRIPS**
300g spinach
150g ricotta
2 medium egg yolks
50g Grana Padano cheese, *grated*

FOR THE FILLING
20–24 quail eggs
about 500ml sunflower oil
1 medium aubergine
'00' flour, *for dusting*
100g peas

TO ASSEMBLE AND SERVE
butter, *for greasing*
1 batch of Tomato Sauce *(see page 272)*
75g pecorino cheese
200g mozzarella cheese *(ideally fior di latte)*

For the béchamel sauce, bring the milk to the boil with a pinch of nutmeg and salt. Meanwhile, melt the butter in a pan over a medium heat. Once melted, add the flour and stir for 2 minutes. Once the milk is ready, add it slowly to the flour mixture ('roux'), stirring constantly with a whisk. Bring the milk to the boil and boil for approximately 5 minutes, then remove from the heat and set aside until ready to use.

To make the meat strips, soak the bread in the milk for 1 minute then squeeze the bread to remove any excess milk. Mix the bread with the parsley and garlic before combining with the beef and veal mince. Add the Grana Padano and sweet paprika, mix well and season with salt and pepper. Roll out the mixture into long sausage-like strips (about 1.5cm thick) and store in the fridge, covered with cling film, until required.

For the spinach and ricotta strips, wash the spinach and transfer the wet leaves to a pan with 1–2 tablespoons of water. Cover with a lid and cook over a medium heat until wilted. Drain and squeeze out any excess water. Using a hand blender, blend the spinach with the ricotta, egg yolks and Grana Padano until just combined, so the spinach still has some texture and is not a complete paste. Transfer the mixture to a piping bag fitted with a 1.5cm round nozzle.

To prepare the other elements of the filling, gently lower the quail eggs into salted boiling water for 4 minutes. Drain and cool in iced water, then peel and cut in half lengthways.

Heat the sunflower oil in a deep saucepan or fat fryer until it reaches 185°C. Cut the aubergine into 1.5cm thick slices, then cut across the slices to make 1.5cm thick strips. Dust the strips with flour and fry the aubergines until nice and golden. Remove and drain on kitchen paper. It is important to coat the aubergines in the flour as this stops the oil getting to the flesh and prevents the aubergines going soggy.

Place the peas in a saucepan and cover with cold water. Season with salt, bring to the boil, then immediately remove from the heat, drain and allow to cool. Set aside until required.

Preheat the oven to 180°C/fan 160°C/gas 4.

To assemble, generously grease a 30 x 20 x 6cm baking dish with butter. Layer the plain pasta sheets across the bottom of the dish, then spread over a third of the tomato sauce, followed by a third of the béchamel to cover it. Running them down the length of the dish, alternate strips of the mince mixture with piped strips of spinach mix, quail eggs and aubergine, until you cover the béchamel.

Add a good sprinkling of grated pecorino on the top, followed by some peas and torn pieces of mozzarella. For the second layer, use the nettle pasta as a base and repeat the process. Top with a layer of white pasta. Cover with the final third of tomato sauce, then béchamel sauce and sprinkle the remaining pecorino over to finish.

Bake for approximately 45 minutes, until golden and bubbling. Remove and leave to cool completely, then transfer to the fridge to set overnight. This step is not essential, you can serve the dish straightaway if you like, but it really benefits from allowing the pasta to settle and the flavours to mature. If you do serve it straightaway, place the dish under a hot grill for a few minutes to brown the top.

The next day, you can either leave the dish to come to room temperature and slice and serve it straightaway – this would be perfect on a summer's day – or you can heat it, in which case heat your oven to 210°C/fan 190°C/gas 7. Slice the set lasagne into portions, place on a baking tray and cook in the oven for approximately 20 minutes or reheat the whole dish for 35–40 minutes. Place under a hot grill for a few minutes to brown the top.

CONCHIGLIONI RIPIENI DI AGNELLO E MAIALE

CONCHIGLIONI STUFFED WITH LAMB AND PORK

CONCHIGLIONI ARE A LARGE SHELL-SHAPED PASTA – they look like seaside conches – and are commonly part-cooked, stuffed then baked in a sauce. Here, their rich, meaty filling and tomato sauce is pure comfort food. Make sure you fill the shells until they're almost bursting - it might seem like a lot of filling but the quantity is just right for the generous stuffing the shells should have.

SERVES 4

24 conchiglioni
1 tsp olive oil
160g Tomato Sauce *(see page 272)*
200g chicken stock
50g pecorino cheese, *grated, plus 2 tbsp to finish*
30g unsalted butter, *melted*
basil leaves, *to garnish*

FOR THE STUFFING

65g stale bread
160ml milk
65g spinach
100g minced lamb
165g minced pork
15g flat-leaf parsley, *roughly chopped*
½ garlic clove, *finely chopped*
1 medium egg
25g pecorino cheese, *grated*
2 mint leaves, *roughly chopped*
½ tsp fresh marjoram, *roughly chopped*
sea salt and freshly ground black pepper

For the stuffing, put the bread and milk in a bowl and leave to soak for about 1 hour, until soft, then remove the bread and squeeze out the liquid (discard the milk). Wash the spinach and transfer the wet leaves to a pan with 1–2 tablespoons of water. Cover with a lid and cook over a medium heat for a few minutes, until wilted. Drain the spinach and squeeze out any excess water, then roughly chop.

Bring a large saucepan of salted water to the boil and cook the conchiglioni for three-quarters of the time suggested on the packet. Drain and put in a large dish mixed with a little olive oil to prevent them sticking and leave to cool.

Preheat the oven to 200°C/fan 180°C/gas 6.

In a bowl, mix the two meats, then add the soaked bread, parsley, garlic, chopped spinach and egg. Mix, then add the pecorino cheese and herbs, season with salt and pepper and mix well. Using a teaspoon, carefully stuff the conchiglioni until very full – the filling should almost burst out as the pasta shells will stretch as they cook.

In a saucepan, mix the tomato sauce with the chicken stock, then pour into the base of a shallow dish which is large enough to fit the conchiglioni in a single layer. Arrange all the stuffed conchiglioni in the sauce. Sprinkle with the pecorino cheese and drizzle over the melted butter. Bake for 30 minutes or until golden on top.

Serve garnished with the basil leaves and extra pecorino cheese.

RISO PATATE E COZZE

IN ITALY, MOST OF THE RICE CROP IS CULTIVATED in the northern regions so rice dishes are associated with the North and are not historically part of my culture. That is changing a little and you will now find risottos served in restaurants in the South, but at home rice was something we were given when we were unwell because it was considered soothing, light and very good for you. This baked rice dish from Bari in Puglia, along with *sartu di riso* from Campania, are the exceptions, and this has become a classic, baked by *mammas* around the country. Somewhere between a paella and a potato gratin, it was originally cooked in a *tiella*, a shallow terracotta dish, over embers. The mussels are the toughest bit to prepare but it's an important step as the juices leaked from the shells will add so much flavour – then you just layer the ingredients in a dish and let the heat from the oven do the rest.

SERVES 4

500g mussels, *cleaned*
2 shallots, *roughly chopped*
3 tbsp extra virgin olive oil
300g vialone nano rice *(or carnaroli if unavailable)*
100ml white wine
150g Cyprus or King Edward potatoes, *peeled and cut into 3mm slices*
10g flat-leaf parsley, *roughly chopped*
5g chives, *roughly chopped*
5g basil leaves, *roughly chopped*
30g pecorino cheese, grated, *plus extra to finish*
100g sun-dried tomatoes
600ml fish stock
sea salt and freshly ground black pepper

Preheat the oven to 210°C / fan 190°C / gas 7.

Start by opening the mussels. There are two muscles holding the flesh inside the shells and you need to cut through the one at the top for the shell to open. Have a bowl ready and start by sliding a small sharp knife into the flat side of one of the mussels. Slide it along the edge to the top until you can feel it cut through the top muscle. Once this is done the shell will open slightly; it just needs to be prised open completely. Scrape the knife around the fish in the top and push it into the bottom part, then snap off the top of the shell and discard. Tip the juices from the shell into the bowl. Repeat with the remainder.

In a large saucepan, sweat the shallots in 1 tablespoon of the oil, until soft, then stir in the rice to coat it in the oil. Pour in the wine, increase the heat to high, and let it evaporate, then remove from the heat, add the reserved mussel juice and set aside to cool a little.

Meanwhile, blanch the potatoes in a small pan of salted boiling water for 2 minutes, then place in a bowl and season with salt, pepper and 1 tablespoon of the olive oil.

Stir the herbs, pecorino cheese and sun-dried tomatoes into the rice. Cover the bottom of a shallow baking dish with half the rice, lay half the mussels on top and cover with a layer of potatoes. Repeat these layers, then pour in enough of the fish stock just to slightly cover the top, season and drizzle with the remaining tablespoon of olive oil. Bake for about 30 minutes, until nice and crunchy on top. Finish with a sprinkle of grated pecorino cheese and leave to rest for 5 minutes before serving.

FREGOLA CANNOLICCHI CARCIOFI E COLATURA

FREGOLA WITH RAZOR CLAMS AND ARTICHOKES

FREGOLA IS A SEMOLA PASTA FROM SARDINIA, often compared to large Israeli couscous. After the simple dough is rolled into small balls, it is left to dry in the sun and then toasted in a large pan, which gives it a deep, nutty taste and a nubbly, rough texture that makes it perfect for soaking up the flavours of sauce and broth.

The island's geography dictates that many of the *fregola* dishes to come out of Sardinia feature seafood and it is typically cooked in a light broth along with the fregola, which locks in all the flavours. Razor clams are a good choice of shellfish because they have a stronger flavour than other varieties but are still sweet and delicate. When you buy razor clams, you will need to check they are still alive and fresh before you cook them. Tap each one gently – the shell should close; if they don't, discard them.

SERVES 4

2 artichokes, *preferably mammole or violet (don't use globe)*
juice of 1 lemon
3 tbsp extra virgin olive oil
½ garlic clove, *finely sliced*
1 long red chilli, *finely sliced*
1 shallot, *roughly chopped*
1 celery stick, *roughly chopped*
100ml white wine
200g fregola
about 300ml fish stock
800g razor clams, *cleaned*
10g mosciame *(see page 50), grated*
4 mint leaves, *finely sliced*

Clean the artichokes by taking off the external leaves until you reach the tender ones. Prepare two bowls of water and divide the lemon juice between the bowls. Pick the tender artichoke leaves one by one and put them into one of the bowls of acidulated water to prevent discolouring. Scoop out the hairy choke with a spoon, slice the artichoke hearts and place in the second bowl. Peel the artichoke stalks, slice them and add to the bowl with the leaves.

In a saucepan, heat 1 tablespoon of the oil with the garlic and chilli over a medium heat. When the garlic is golden, add the shallot and celery and sweat until softened, then drain the artichoke hearts, stalks and leaves and add them to the pan. Increase the heat to high and fry for 1 minute, then pour in the wine and leave to evaporate. Add the fregola, stir for 1 minute then pour in the fish stock, cover with the lid and simmer for about 5 minutes. Add the razor clams and cook for 4–5 minutes or until the shells open (discard any that haven't). Add a little more stock if needed – the consistency should be more like a broth than a risotto.

When the fregola is tender but still with a little bite, remove from the heat and stir through the grated mosciame, the remaining 2 tablespoons of oil and the mint. Cover with cling film and leave it to rest for a couple of minutes before serving.

3

PESCE

CERNIA OLIVE E ROSMARINO

GROUPER WITH OLIVES AND ROSEMARY

I ASSOCIATE THIS DISH WITH CELEBRATIONS. In the South you will often find it served after weddings and baptisms and as grouper can grow until they're extremely large, it's not unusual to see fish weighing as much as 30 or 40 kilograms being pulled out of the oven. The olive oil and white wine keep the fish beautifully moist and the flesh will just fall off the bone. Traditionally, the whole fish is placed in front of the head of the table for him or her to serve and it's accompanied by just a selection of salads and vegetables.

Grouper is a beautiful white-fleshed fish from the same family as sea bass. It thrives in warm water and is therefore considered an 'exotic' fish but sadly one that is vulnerable to overfishing using methods that are detrimental to their habitat. Please be very careful how you source your grouper – you need to make sure you're buying sustainably farmed fish. This is definitely a dish for special occasions.

SERVES 4

1kg grouper, *gutted and scaled*
300g fennel, *trimmed and cut into wedges*
250ml fish stock
100ml white wine
30g pitted black olives
10g rosemary
2 tbsp extra virgin olive oil
10g capers
6 white peppercorns
sea salt

Preheat the oven to 200°C / fan 180°C / gas 6.

Season the grouper with salt and place in a deep baking dish. Arrange the fennel wedges around the fish then add all the remaining ingredients.

Bake the fish for about 25 minutes. Check the thickest part – it should flake easily.

When the fish is cooked, transfer it to a serving dish, then pour over any cooking juice.

ROMBO AL FORNO

BAKED TURBOT WITH POTATO AND CHERRY TOMATOES

THE TOMATOES IN THIS DISH POINT TO ITS ORIGINS:
you'll find it served around Naples and the Amalfi coast. There it would traditionally be cooked in a wood-fired oven (after the pizzas!), which gives it a slightly smoky flavour. It is a colourful one-pot dish that's very much about sharing; it is simply placed in the middle of the table and everybody helps themselves. That said, turbot is quite a luxurious and expensive fish to buy, in Italy as well as in the UK, and there are certain rules about who gets to eat which part of the fish. The head of the house serves themself the cheeks, which are considered the best as they're the most tender, while everybody else gets the fillet. The children are also given the eyes. I know this might sound strange but they're actually delicious, and as kids we used to love sucking the white to get to the clear pearl inside. If you've never tried them I'd highly recommend you do.

SERVES 4

800g Cyprus potatoes, *peeled and cut into 5mm slices*
220g cherry tomatoes, *halved*
150g Tropea red onions, *cut into 5mm slices*
30g salted capers, *soaked overnight*
160g Moroccan dry black olives
10g thyme
75ml extra virgin olive oil
1 turbot, *about 2.2kg*
175ml white wine
sea salt and freshly ground black pepper

Preheat the oven to 220°C / fan 200°C / gas 7.

Drop the potatoes into a pan of salted boiling water and blanch for 1 minute. Drain and set aside in a bowl to cool, mixed with a little olive oil.

Put the cherry tomatoes, onion, capers, black olives, thyme and olive oil into a bowl. Season with salt and pepper.

Season the turbot with salt and place it in a large roasting tray. Spread the vegetable mixture on top, then arrange the potatoes around the fish and pour over the wine.

Bake the fish for 25–30 minutes or until the flesh is opaque and just cooked through (it should come away from the bone easily).

AGGHIOTTA DI PESCE SPADA

OVEN-BAKED SWORDFISH

A TRADITIONAL SICILIAN DISH from the area around the town of Messina, where some of the region's finest swordfish is caught, '*Agghiotta*' is actually an Italianised translation of the Sicilian '*a ghiotta*', which means 'for the glutton'. There are different takes on how gluttonous to make the recipe – sometimes the fish is fried first and according to a Sicilian's preference it may include raisins and pine nuts, but my cooking method and ingredients keep it simple and I think it still lives up to its title. You could also cook the fish in a covered barbecue, which will give it a beautiful smoky flavour. Lay a few rosemary or sage sprigs on the grill to add extra aromas.

SERVES 4

700g swordfish fillet, *cut into large chunks*
2 Tropea onions, *sliced into rounds*
16 cherry tomatoes, *quartered*
8 salted anchovy fillets, *rinsed and roughly chopped*
2 tbsp capers
16 green olives, *pitted*
50ml extra virgin olive oil
2 tbsp Tomato Sauce *(see page 272)*
1 tbsp flat-leaf parsley, *roughly chopped*
1 tbsp basil, *roughly chopped*
1 tsp dried oregano
125ml dry white wine
sea salt and freshly ground black pepper, *to taste*

Mix all the ingredients in a bowl, then transfer to a baking dish and set aside to marinate for 30 minutes.

Preheat the oven to 220°C / fan 200°C / gas 7.

When the oven is hot, bake the swordfish for 25 minutes, until piping hot and cooked through.

This is absolutely beautiful served with creamy crushed potatoes with olive oil, or for something simpler, some bruschetta drizzled with olive oil.

GAMBERONI ARROSTO SU MACCO DI CECI E ANICE NERO

ROAST KING PRAWNS WITH CHICKPEA MASH

THE MOORISH INFLUENCE on the history of southern Italy is still very evident in much of our cooking and if I were to try and describe this dish I would say, imagine a hummus with some king prawns as your dipper. It's the fennel and tomatoes that root the dish in Italy and my touch is to add a splash of dry Marsala wine to sweeten the prawns and the sauce.

You will make more prawn stock than you need but it freezes well and can be kept for up to a month.

SERVES 4

20 raw king prawns, *in their shells*
½ shallot, *roughly chopped*
20g fennel, *roughly chopped*
2 tbsp extra virgin olive oil
¼ tsp tomato purée
¼ tsp anise seeds or fennel seeds
1kg ice cubes
sunflower oil, *for deep-frying*
120g cherry tomatoes, *halved*
100g Savoy cabbage, *leaves separated*
1 red chilli, *halved, deseeded and cut lengthways into fine strips*
4 tsp Greco di Bianco or Marsala wine
5g dill
fine sea salt and freshly ground black pepper

FOR THE CHICKPEA MASH

175g chickpeas, *soaked overnight in cold water*
½ shallot, *roughly chopped*
20g peeled carrot, *roughly chopped*
20g trimmed celery, *roughly chopped*
½ tsp black anise seeds

For the chickpea mash, put the chickpeas into a casserole with the shallot, carrot and celery. Pour in just enough water to cover, bring to the boil, then simmer for about 1–2 hours until they are tender but still have a slight bite. Add a few pinches of fine salt.

Peel and devein the prawns but leave the heads and tails on. In a saucepan, sweat the shallot and fennel in 1 tablespoon of olive oil, add the prawn shells and toast for 1 minute, then add the tomato purée, the anise or fennel seeds, then cover with the ice. (Using ice cubes for the stock is a good trick as they will take a lot longer to come to the boil than water does, which means the shells have more time to release their flavour.) Bring to the boil and cook for 45 minutes.

Remove from the heat, leave to cool then pass through a sieve. Reheat just before you continue with the chickpea mash.

Remove a couple of heaped tablespoons of chickpeas (no liquid) and set aside. Add the black anise seeds to the pan of chickpeas, then transfer the pan's contents to a food processor and blend until you have a smooth but thick purée. Add 50ml of the prawn stock if it's too thick, check the seasoning and adjust the salt.

Start to heat a deep saucepan or fat fryer with sunflower oil until the oil reaches 170°C. Heat an overhead grill to high.

Place the cherry tomatoes, cut-side up, on a baking tray and grill until browned, then set aside.

continued overleaf

Deep-fry the reserved chickpeas until crispy, then remove with a slotted spoon and drain on kitchen paper.

In salted boiling water, blanch the cabbage leaves for 1 minute then place in iced water to cool.

Heat a frying pan with 1 tablespoon of olive oil over a medium–high heat, cook the prawns in batches, searing them on each side until pink and just cooked through, and adding more oil as necessary. Remove and set aside.

Drain the cabbage leaves well then add them to the pan and sear for 1 minute on each side, then add the chilli and season with salt and pepper. Pour in the wine, allow to evaporate over a high heat then add enough of the prawn stock to get a creamy sauce.

Transfer the prawns to a warm serving dish, top with the grilled tomatoes and sauce and garnish with the dill. Serve the chickpea mash and cabbage in a separate serving dish, topped with the crunchy chickpeas.

BACCALÀ MARINATO ALLA LIQUIRIZIA

COD MARINATED IN LIQUORICE

'BACCALÀ', OR SALT COD (not to be confused with dried cod, which is very different), is not considered particularly glamorous. Historically it was food for the poor as it was cheap and in abundant supply – the salt cure preserved the fish so it could be kept for several months. However, the salting has another practical side: cod flesh is very flaky but salting keeps it firm so that it holds its shape when cooked.

Salt cod is typically soaked for about 3 days to rinse off all the salt but in this recipe I've made my life – and yours – easier, so I've lightly salted plain cod fillet myself for just 3 hours so that it still has that beautiful firm flesh but you don't have to wait for it (or have the smell of the salty fish in your house). I then marinate it in three different types of liquorice: sticks, for their bitter aroma, powder for its sweetness, and liqueur, which softens and partially cooks the fish (for more on liquorice see page 237). With a final punch from the red chilli and a touch of luxury from the Prosecco, for me this is a perfect dish.

SERVES 4

900g black cod fillet, *with skin*
70g coarse sea salt
30g fine sea salt

FOR THE MARINADE
50ml dry Prosecco
100ml liquorice liqueur
3 liquorice sticks
½ tsp liquorice powder
25g clear honey
1 red chilli, *halved*

Remove any bones from the cod fillet, place in a shallow dish and cover it with a mixture of the two salts. Set aside for 45 minutes.

Meanwhile, in a shallow dish large enough to hold the cod flat, mix together all the ingredients for the marinade.

Rinse the cod with cold water then pat dry and place in the marinade. Turn the fish several times to ensure it is well coated, then leave to marinate for about 12 hours.

Preheat the oven to 200°C/fan 180°C/gas 6. Drain the cod from the marinade and place in a roasting tin lined with baking paper. Bake for about 5 minutes until slightly pink in the middle then place under a very hot grill for about 3 minutes to finish the cooking – watch it carefully to make sure it doesn't burn. Serve immediately.

Clockwise from top left:
salted sardines,
anchovy fillets in oil,
grey mullet bottarga,
collatura di alici.

CONSERVE DI PESCE

PRESERVED FISH

IT IS THOUGHT THAT NO POINT IN ITALY lies farther than 120km from a coastline, so it follows that we should have a food culture heavily reliant on the sea. Preserving fish did, of course, begin out of necessity – drying, curing, salting, pickling and smoking were all ways of ensuring a glut could be stored for leaner times. Today, the need is not as present, but the tradition of preserving seafood has continued, and certain types of preserved fish can be more expensive and sought after than fresh.

There seems to be quite a love–hate relationship with anchovies in this country. Some people relish the flavour of the salty, oily fish, and the depth it can bring to cooking, but all too often I see anchovies relegated to pizza toppings (and I've watched diners fastidiously pick each one off), or gingerly folded through salads as a token ingredient. In Italy, however, anchovies are indispensable – worshipped almost. We have a strong culture of using *acciuge*, or *alici* as they are also called, in every region and in all parts of our cooking. In fact our relationship and love of the small blue fish dates from the Roman times – archaeological digs at Pompei have unearthed amphoras full of anchovy bones, which were used in their preparation of *garum* (more on this below).

Fresh anchovies are commonly found on the coast, where they are cooked in a similar way to sardines – often on the grill, but when I talk about using anchovies in our cooking, I'm really referring to the use of preserved anchovies. In Italy, and in Spain, which also has a strong heritage in preserving fish, anchovies are washed in brine, dried, filleted and packed into tins or jars of salt, or, as you're most likely to find them in the UK, olive oil. In Calabria, I buy the salted anchovies, soaking them overnight before using them, but in the UK these are difficult to come by and there are two brands of anchovies preserved in extra virgin olive oil, one from Italy (Callipo) and one from Spain (Ortiz), which are excellent. As with so many ingredients, if you're prepared to spend a little more, you get a very good quality product so do try and buy the best you can afford. And of course, as with all my cooking, no part of an ingredient is wasted, so I use everything – the oil from the tin can be used in place of standard olive oil, and the salt can be used for seasoning.

In the *mezzogiorno* region, the king of all forms of preserved anchovy, and the one I could

WHEN I TALK ABOUT USING ANCHOVIES IN OUR COOKING, I'M REALLY REFERRING TO THE USE OF PRESERVED ANCHOVIES

not live without, is *garum*. The term is now used to describe a range of fermented fish sauces, but it was originally conceived by the Romans, who began fermenting fish to create a liquid or paste, which they used as a condiment. *Garum*, or *liquamen* as similar forms were known, became as important to classical cooking as salt is to us today. A mixture of oily fish and / or their discarded parts were mixed with salt then either packed into barrels or left to dry in the sun. After a few weeks, a fishy liquid was drawn off then stored in amphoras. Today, the *garum* that most resembles the original Roman invention is *colatura di alici*, which means 'filtering of anchovies'. *Colatura di alici*, which now enjoys PDO status, is produced in the town of Cetara on the Amalfi Coast in Campania.

The anchovies are gutted and have their heads removed before being layered with salt inside chestnut barrels. They're weighed down and left for at least 5 months, then a small hole

IN THE *MEZZOGIORNO* REGION, THE KING OF ALL FORMS OF PRESERVED ANCHOVY, AND THE ONE I COULD NOT LIVE WITHOUT, IS *GARUM*

is made in the bottom of the barrel. The first water to be released stinks and is discarded, but slowly the treasured amber-coloured liquid starts to drop. It is one of the most amazing things. It is like a Thai fish sauce, but with a more rounded and delicate flavour because it has the purity of being made from a single fish rather than a mixture. Sadly it's very difficult to find *colatura di alici* in the UK, but if you do ever find yourself in Italy with room in your suitcase, it's really worth picking up a bottle (it will last for months in the fridge).

Aside from *colatura di alici*, you can buy *garum* in two forms – as anchovy water, and as a paste. Throughout the book I've used only the liquid form, but as you'll see, it's an integral part of my cooking. Like the *colatura*, liquid *garum* is like a more elegant and milder form of an Asian fish sauce. It works beautifully in pasta sauces and light marinades and it can lift a simple steamed green vegetable, such as broccoli, like

you wouldn't believe. It's very strong so you only need a small amount, and the more you play with it, the more you'll learn how to use it and how much suits your taste. Slice a mozzarella ball in half, add a drizzle of extra virgin olive oil and a teaspoon of *garum* and you'll see what I mean; it makes an amazing dressing in itself. A *spaghetti alle vongole* will be transformed as will a *puttanesca* or any other seafood-based pasta sauce. If you buy it in the UK, you are going to have to go to an Italian delicatessen, but I promise you the trip will pay off as you only use it in very small quantities and it can be kept in the fridge for months.

The thicker *garum* paste is made from either red mullet, mackerel and sardines or a combination. The fermented fish is cooked with spices and some tomato paste then squeezed through a muslin to make a paste. The paste is good for a fish soup but it has a very strong smell and is not something I cook with often.

Sardinia and Sicily are known for preserving fish roe. In Sardinia, it is taken from grey mullet *(mugine)*, which are plentiful in the waters around the island; while in Sicily it is more commonly tuna *(tonno)*. The egg sacks are very gently and carefully removed from the fish, so as not to pierce any eggs, then they are salted and pressed into the characteristic oblong shapes, before being left in the sun to dry for 1 – 4 months. *Bottarga di mugine* can be anything from an amber to a deep brown colour and is waxy and firm. Frankly, in its block state, it does not look particularly appetising but sliced or grated, the deeply savoury fishy flavour it adds to dishes is extraordinary. If you're new to bottarga the best way to try it is with a very simple pasta dish, such as the linguine with garlic, oil and bottarga on page 87, but the flavour also works beautifully with vegetables, particularly bitter greens, such as the turnip tops with bottarga on page 178.

TRIGLIE GRIGLIATE AL SALMORIGLIO

GRILLED RED MULLET WITH SALMORIGLIO

SALMORIGLIO IS TRADITIONALLY A SICILIAN MARINADE, but it's now become common all over Italy, where it's often served as a sauce with grilled meat and all kinds of fish. The essential ingredients are the lemon juice, olive oil, oregano and garlic but the rest are open to interpretation; this is my version.

This recipe reminds me of going to the seaside as a child. Southern Italians generally bring half their house to the beach, particularly when it comes to mealtimes, and my family was no exception. My mum would often unpack a warm lasagne, salads, bread and wine as well as this beautiful marinated fish, which is still one of my favourites. It's actually perfect for a beach lunch as the fish is just very lightly grilled then left to continue cooking in its marinade as it cools to room temperature, which is how it's best served. You could swap the red mullet for grey or for mackerel or sardines, depending on your taste.

SERVES 4

12 small red mullet *(approximately 130g each)*, *scaled and gutted*
3 garlic cloves, *sliced*
10g marjoram, *roughly chopped*
10g thyme, *roughly chopped*
10g rosemary, *roughly chopped*
2 tsp dried oregano
30g dried chilli, *roughly chopped*
4 tbsp Cabernet Sauvignon vinegar
200ml extra virgin olive oil
½ tsp fennel seeds
1 tbsp clear honey
pared zest and juice of 1 lemon
1 tsp sea salt
10ml mosto cotto (balsamic syrup)
10 tinned anchovies
4 tsp garum (anchovy water)

Wash the fish and dry on kitchen paper.

For the salmoriglio, put all the remaining ingredients into a bowl and quickly mix with a whisk or a spoon. Pass through a sieve and set aside.

Heat your oven grill on high until very hot. Grill the red mullet for 1 minute on each side then transfer to an oven set at 200°C / fan 180°C / gas 6 for 3 minutes, then immediately remove – it will continue to cook as it cools so you don't want to overcook it at this stage.

Transfer to a serving dish and pour over the sauce. Leave the fish to cool completely then serve at room temperature.

TONNO E FINOCCHIO AL FORNO

BAKED FENNEL AND TUNA

TUNA 'MEATBALLS' are found all over southern Italy and Sicily. They are a beautiful dish as they stand, but I wanted to have a little fun with my version and make the meatballs a little more unusual. I've stuffed a minced tuna mixture into fennel and baked them in the oven, which makes them a little more 'Francesco'. There is also a very practical reason for cooking the fish this way. Tuna is very lean, which means it can easily turn dry, but here the fennel shells release their own juices during the cooking and keep it nice and moist. It's so hot in the South that I would serve this at room temperature, with just a squeeze of lemon, but you can serve it all year round, straight out of the oven or however you like.

SERVES 4

100g crustless sourdough bread or other
    coarse-textured bread
200ml milk
400g tuna loin, *cut into 3mm cubes*
¼ red onion, *finely chopped*
¼ garlic clove
5g dill
1kg fennel
3 tbsp extra virgin olive oil
1 small shallot, *finely chopped*
60g tinned anchovy fillets, *drained, rinsed*
    and chopped
100ml white wine
generous pinch of saffron strands
2 courgettes, *cut into 3mm dice, plus 2*
    courgette flowers
15g salted capers, *soaked overnight then drained*
40g black pitted olives
200ml fish stock
sea salt and freshly ground black pepper

Preheat the oven to 200°C/fan 180°C/gas 6. Soak the bread in the milk.

Put the tuna into a bowl and add the red onion, garlic and dill. Squeeze the bread to remove the milk and add to the tuna. Season with salt and pepper and mix well.

Trim the base of each fennel bulb and detach the leaves. Discard the first two thicker leaves, remove the core and reserve. Depending on the size of the fennel, you will use four large ones or eight small ones. Blanch the hollowed out fennel in salted boiling water for 3–4 minutes, then drain and transfer to a bowl of iced water to cool. Drain the fennel and dry thoroughly, then fill with the tuna mix and set aside.

Cut the reserved fennel cores into 3mm dice. In a large ovenproof casserole, heat 1 tablespoon of the olive oil over a medium heat and sweat the shallot and anchovies until the onion is soft – about 5 minutes – then add the fennel dice and sweat for another minute. Pour in the wine and over a medium–high heat let it evaporate. Add the saffron, courgette dice and their flowers, capers, olives and fish stock and bring to the boil, then remove from the heat.

Heat a frying pan with 2 tablespoons of olive oil over a medium heat and fry the filled fennel tuna-side down until the tuna is sealed and browned. Transfer the fennel to the sauce and push them into it so that they are submerged about halfway. Transfer the casserole to the oven and cook for 10–15 minutes or until the tuna is cooked through and the fennel is soft – it will depend on the size of the fennel.

TAGLIATA DI TONNO

TUNA TAGLIATA WITH MIXED PEPPER SALAD

'TAGLIATA' MEANS SLICED, and though you may be more familiar with
the beef version – essentially the Italian way to serve tender beef fillet, which
is found all over the country, this sliced tuna loin uses the same principles of
the dish. The tuna is seared quickly over a very high heat leaving it pink in the
middle, then it is sliced and served on top of a simple marinated pepper salad.
It's a wonderful, light summery dish and so easy to prepare.

SERVES 4

40g sultanas
3 mixed peppers (1 red; 1 yellow; 1 green)
4 tbsp extra virgin olive oil, *for brushing and
    drizzling*
3 tbsp red wine vinegar
5g dill, *roughly chopped*
500g tuna loin
½ tsp fennel pollen
20g pistachios, *toasted*
rock salt

Soak the sultanas in water overnight.

On a very hot griddle pan or barbecue, grill the peppers until the
skins are blistered and blackened. Transfer to a container, cover
with cling film and leave to steam. After about 20 minutes, scrape off
and discard the blackened skin. Pierce each pepper and allow the juice
to drain into a bowl. Remove and discard the seed pod, stem and
inner ribs.

Cut the peppers into thin slices and place in a serving bowl. Drain
the sultanas and add to the peppers with the olive oil, vinegar, dill
and reserved juice from the peppers.

Heat a large frying pan over a high heat. Brush the tuna with olive oil,
sprinkle over the fennel pollen and a pinch of rock salt. Sear the tuna
until browned and seared on all sides.

Cut the tuna into 5mm-thick slices and place on top of the pepper
and sultana salad.

Scatter over the pistachios, drizzle with more olive oil and scatter
with rock salt.

SEPPIE AL NERO E BERGAMOTTO

CUTTLEFISH AND BERGAMOT

THIS DISH IS BASED ON A LOCAL FISHERMEN'S PRIVILEGE.
When anglers landed their boats, they would take the small cuttlefish from the
catch, remove the ink sac, then place the cuttlefish in a box with some pebbles
and gently rock and rattle the stones until the cuttlefish turned slightly curly.
They would then rinse it with sea water before seasoning it with olive oil,
bergamot juice and zest, chilli and parsley, toss it in enough black ink to colour
it, then eat it raw. The strong zesty aroma of the bergamot was used to hide
the pungent smell of the salty sea water.

For those of us that aren't brave enough to eat cuttlefish raw, here I've
taken the essence of the dish but have quickly pan-fried the cuttlefish and
balanced it with the acidity and fragrance of the citrus rather than drowning it.

Cuttlefish are really messy to prepare because they contain so much ink,
so unless you want to end up with a very black kitchen I would suggest you
ask your fishmonger to do the prep for you and to give you the sac of ink.
Alternatively they should also sell pasteurised ink.

SERVES 4

1 tbsp extra virgin olive oil
1 white onion, *finely chopped*
1 red chilli, *finely chopped*
8–10 sage leaves, *finely chopped*
2 cuttlefish *(about 1.6kg), cleaned and prepared
– body and tentacles separated (ask your
fishmonger to do this for you and to give you
the ink sac, see above)*
125ml white wine
2 sachets squid ink, *(optional; see above)*
20g flat-leaf parsley, *roughly chopped*
grated zest and juice of 1 bergamot *(see page 85)*
sea salt and freshly ground black pepper

Heat a frying pan, add the olive oil and sweat the onion, chilli and
sage over a medium heat until softened. Add the cuttlefish, as well
as the wine, and season well. Simmer until the liquid has reduced
completely.

Remove the cuttlefish and slice the body into very fine strips (leave
the tentacles whole), then return to the sauce along with a tablespoon
of ink. Cover and cook for 1 hour on a very low heat. There should
be enough liquid but if it looks as if the pan is getting dry, add a
little water.

Take the sauce off the heat and stir through the parsley and bergamot
before serving.

CALAMARI RIPIENI

STUFFED CALAMARI

THIS IS A BEAUTIFUL, FRESH, SIMPLE DISH, which my mum cooks as part of a big Sunday lunch. Stuffing things is a particularly southern trait and this recipe is now something of a southern Italian classic, but the squid would most likely originally have been stuffed more humbly just with pecorino and breadcrumbs. Here I've mixed things up a bit. The herbs add freshness even though the squid is cooked for a long time, while the peas and pepper bulk out the filling to make it more of a substantial main course. Play around with the stuffing and add cheese if you like – pecorino and ricotta both work well – and make sure there's plenty of crusty Italian bread for scooping up all the tomato sauce.

SERVES 4

120g frozen petit pois
20 medium squid *(around 1.6kg), cleaned and gutted but keep the tentacles (ask your fishmonger to do this for you)*
3 medium egg whites
200g Romano peppers, *cut into 5mm dice*
10g chives, *chopped*
20 sturdy rosemary sprigs *(optional)*
1 garlic clove, *with skin, halved*
1 tbsp extra virgin olive oil
100ml white wine
400ml Tomato Sauce *(see page 272)*
250ml fish stock

Preheat the oven to 200°C / fan 180°C / gas 6. Blanch the peas in boiling water for 30 seconds, then drain well.

Put 8 of the squid and the egg whites into a food processor and pulse until they are roughly chopped. Add the peppers, blanched peas and chives and continue to pulse until you have a coarse mixture.

Use this mixture to stuff the remaining calamari, keeping some space free at the top. Place a piece of the tentacles at the end of the filling and close the calamari with a rosemary sprig or a toothpick. Trim the other end of each calamari to create a tiny hole and keep the filling from bursting out when cooking.

Heat a large heatproof baking dish over a medium heat and fry the garlic in 1 tablespoon of olive oil. Add the calamari and fry for a couple of minutes until browned, then pour in the wine and let it evaporate over a medium–high heat. Add the tomato sauce and the fish stock, then transfer to the oven for 20 minutes. You can check the filling is cooked through by sticking a toothpick in the centre of the filling; it should feel hot when you touch your lips. Serve immediately.

CODA DI ROSPO AL CIRÒ, PANCETTA E LENTICCHIE DI ROTONDA

MONKFISH WITH CIRÒ WINE, PANCETTA AND ROTONDA LENTILS

CIRÒ WINE is produced on the mountainous east coast of Calabria. It is thought to be one of the oldest wines in the world and is certainly Calabria's finest. Cirò is largely made up of the *gaglioppo* grape, the region's main variety, which is known for producing soft red wines with a gentle berry flavour. It's very easy to drink so you can even enjoy it without food. There are very few fish dishes in southern Italy that are cooked in red wine – this one was probably left to us by the French – but here the robust monkfish flesh really does benefit from the lightness of the Cirò without being overpowered by it. The wine is gently reduced, yet it never becomes too sweet. It colours the fish a beautiful purple and provides a delicate balance for the earthy lentils and pancetta. This is hearty, rustic comfort food, with a touch of southern sunshine thrown in too.

SERVES 4

200g Rotonda, Castellucio or Puy lentils
720–750g monkfish tail *(ask your fishmonger to give you the bone)*
100g pancetta *(ideally in a single piece)*
½ leek, *white part only, chopped*
1 tbsp tomato purée
1 bay leaf
80g red onion, *finely diced*
1–2 tbsp extra virgin olive oil
2 tsp sugar
4 tsp red wine vinegar
250ml Cirò red wine
2 tbsp '00' flour
50ml port
5g dill, *roughly chopped*
sea salt and freshly ground black pepper

Put the lentils, monkfish bone, pancetta, leek, tomato purée and bay leaf into a large saucepan. Cover with double the quantity of water, bring to the boil, then lower the heat and simmer for about 40–45 minutes until the lentils are tender but still have a slight bite. Lift out the fish bone and bay leaf and discard.

Remove the pancetta piece, cut it into 5mm dice and leave aside. Take out a third of the lentils with some of their liquid and use a hand blender to purée them until smooth then return them to the pan with the remainder, being sure there is not too much liquid in it – it should feel and look like a thick soup. If it's very thick, stir in more water (around 100ml) to loosen it. Cover and set aside.

Put the red onion into a small saucepan with a tablespoon of the olive oil, the sugar and a pinch of salt. Place the pan over a very low heat and cover with a lid. Start to sweat the red onion, then add the vinegar. Allow to evaporate, then add 50ml of the red wine and let it cook, still covered, until the onion has softened but is still a little bit crunchy – about 5 minutes.

Cut the monkfish into 50–60g medallions, season with salt and pepper and dust with the flour.

Preheat the oven to 200°C/fan 180°C/gas 6.

Heat an ovenproof casserole and fry the pancetta over a medium heat with 1 teaspoon of oil until browned and crispy. Lift it out and drain on kitchen paper. In the same pan, fry the monkfish medallions on each side, in batches, adding another teaspoon of olive oil if necessary, until browned and sealed, then set aside on a plate. Pour in the remaining red wine and the port, increase the heat to high and simmer for a minute or two to let the alcohol evaporate. Stir in the red onion then put the fish medallions back into the pan, along with any juices on the plate. Cover the casserole then transfer it to the oven and cook for about 8–9 minutes or until the fish is cooked through (the cooking time depends on the size of your medallions).

While the fish is in the oven, reheat the lentils gently until hot. Stir through the pancetta then transfer them to a warm serving dish and lay the monkfish medallions on top. Pour over the red onion sauce from the casserole and finish by scattering over the dill.

CUCCIATA E BRODETTO DI PESCE

COUSCOUS AND FISH BROTH

COUSCOUS isn't a food one normally associates with Italy, but this firmly Sicilian dish proves that southern Italy has a very strong Moorish heritage and that food still intimately ties the two sides of the Mediterranean. If you go to Tunisia you're very likely to encounter a north African version of a spaghetti with tomato and basil, while in Sicily, the fine corn-yellow wheat grain is very much a staple ingredient. It's a happy melding of cultures and makes for some interesting gastronomic experiences. This fish broth lacks the spices you'd undoubtedly find in a north African couscous dish, but instead there are fresh herbs, wine and tomato, which is where the Sicilians come in.

SERVES 4

500g prepared cuttlefish (body and tentacles; ask your fishmonger to prepare it for you)
20g shallots, chopped
1 garlic clove, sliced
1 red chilli, deseeded and sliced
1 thyme sprig
2 tbsp extra virgin olive oil
50ml white wine
1 tbsp tomato purée
about 1.5 litres prawn or fish stock
200g couscous
300g clams, cleaned
300g mussels, cleaned
15g flat-leaf parsley, roughly chopped
10g basil, roughly chopped
5g dill, roughly chopped
5g chives, roughly chopped
1 tarragon sprig, roughly chopped
sea salt and freshly ground black pepper

Wash the cuttlefish and cut it into cubes of about 1cm and set aside.

In the meantime, put the shallot, garlic, chilli and thyme into a saucepan with the olive oil and fry until the shallot and garlic are golden brown. Add the cuttlefish and let it cook on a high heat for a couple of minutes. Pour in the white wine and let it evaporate. Season with salt, then add the tomato purée and enough stock to cover. Simmer until the cuttlefish are tender, adding more stock if needed so that it stays submerged.

Meanwhile, cover the couscous with 150ml of salted boiling water, stir, add a few drops of olive oil, cover with cling film and leave for 5 minutes. When ready to serve, use a fork to separate the grains then place in a steamer for a few minutes or microwave to reheat.

Add the clams and mussels to the cuttlefish, cover with a lid and cook on a high heat for about 2 minutes, shaking the pan occasionally, until the clams and mussels all open (discard any that don't), then remove from the heat.

Finish by stirring through the chopped herbs and check the seasoning. Serve with the warm couscous on the side.

POLPO IN UMIDO

STEWED OCTOPUS

DON'T BE INTIMIDATED BY OCTOPUS; it's actually very easy to prepare and cook and once you get over any squeamishness you might have about eating tentacles you will discover a rich, meaty seafood that is tender and perfect for hearty stews. Octopus flesh is very tough so before you do anything with it you need to tenderise it. One way to do this is to bash the octopus against a hard surface – that's what a fisherman would do, which is thought to cause its muscles to relax, but an easier way to do this is to buy frozen octopus and defrost it, which has the same effect. Cooking it slowly will also tenderise it further.

SERVES 6 — 8

1.5kg frozen octopus, *defrosted overnight*
2 tbsp extra virgin olive oil
500g red onions, *finely sliced*
3 dried chillies
125ml red wine
4 tsp red wine vinegar
1 × 50g tin anchovy fillets
1 tsp brown sugar
500g mixed peppers
3 spring onions, *roughly chopped*
small handful of flat-leaf parsley, *roughly chopped*

Cut the octopus body from the tentacles and slice between the tentacles to separate them. Cut the body into 5–6 pieces.

Place 1 tablespoon of olive oil in a large casserole and fry the chunks in batches over a medium heat, until the flesh turns from grey to purple – this should only take up to a minute per batch. Set aside in a large bowl after each batch is done.

Add the onion to the pan with the remaining tablespoon of oil and cook over a medium heat for 5–10 minutes, until softened. Add the chillies, wine, vinegar, anchovies and sugar. Stir well then spoon the octopus into the pan together with any juices from the bowl. Cover and bring to a simmer. Turn the heat down to low and cook, covered, for 1 hour, or until the octopus is tender.

On a very hot griddle pan or barbecue, grill the peppers until the skins are blistered and charred. Transfer to a container, cover with cling film and leave to steam and cool. After about 20 minutes, remove the blackened skin, stem and seed pod. Slice into large pieces.

Remove the octopus from the pan with a slotted spoon and set aside. Turn the heat up to medium and allow the liquid to bubble to reduce it, until the onions are nicely caramelised.

To serve, arrange the peppers on a plate with the octopus chunks and onions on top and drizzle some of the reduced cooking liquid around. Serve with the spring onion and parsley scattered over the top.

4
CARNE

POLLO E BUCATINI

WHOLE ROAST CHICKEN STUFFED WITH BUCATINI

A FUSION OF ITALIAN AND BRITISH FAVOURITES – roast chicken stuffed with strands of long, thin rolls of pasta; surely a fantastic combination? It is in fact an old recipe, one that is served on special occasions, traditionally as the main course on Christmas Day, but it's quite unusual to see it served these days, mainly because boning the chicken is quite a fiddly job. You can ask your butcher to do it for you, but bear in mind that it will take them a while so thank them!

Sealing the chicken cavity with rosemary sprigs adds flavour to the meat so don't skip this step if you can find sturdy rosemary.

SERVES 6

1 banana shallot, *roughly chopped*
4 tsp extra virgin olive oil
200g unsmoked sliced pancetta
150ml white wine
200ml Tomato Sauce *(see page 272)*
150ml chicken stock
100g fresh peas
120g bucatini
5g flat-leaf parsley, *roughly chopped*
5g chives, *roughly chopped*
50g pecorino cheese, *grated*
100g mozzarella cheese, *cut into small cubes*
1 chicken, *about 1.8 kg (boned; ask your very kind butcher to do this for you)*
sea salt and freshly ground black pepper

You will also need some rosemary sprigs or skewers to seal the chicken

Preheat the oven to 180°C / fan 160°C / gas 4.

In a frying pan over a medium heat, sweat the shallot in the oil for 5 – 10 minutes until soft but not coloured.

Cut half the pancetta into matchsticks and add them to the pan. Increase the heat to high and continue to fry until the pancetta is nice and crispy (but be careful not to burn the shallot). Pour in the wine, allow it to evaporate, then add the tomato sauce and the chicken stock. Cook on a medium heat for 5 minutes, then add the peas and simmer for 5 minutes more, then turn off the heat.

Meanwhile, bring a pan of salted water to the boil, add the bucatini and cook for half the time suggested on the packet. Drain and mix into the sauce, then stir in the parsley, chives and pecorino cheese. Remove from the heat and leave to cool. It needs to cool quickly so that it doesn't continue cooking, so spread the mixture out in a tray. Once cool stir through the mozzarella.

Season the chicken with salt and pepper, then place in a bowl and stuff it with the pasta and sauce. Seal the end by securing the back skin together with rosemary sprigs or toothpicks, then remove from the bowl and tie the legs and wings together with kitchen string. Finally cover the whole chicken with the remaining pancetta slices.

Bake in the oven for 30 – 40 minutes then increase the temperature to 200°C / fan 180°C / gas 6 and cook at this heat for 10 – 15 minutes until it's nice and crispy and the juices run clear when a skewer is pushed into the thickest part of the breast. Leave to rest for 5 – 10 minutes (not covered) then slice and serve.

QUAGLIE MARINATE ARROSTO

ROAST MARINATED QUAIL

IF THE SUN SHINES and you find yourself with a sunny weekend, this is such a great dish for a barbecue – it's how I would always cook it in South Italy. Marinate the quail on Saturday night and get your friends round for a barbecue the next day. Serve it with some simple salads or vegetables from the Vegetali and Antipasti chapters (see pages 176 and 20) and you've got a beautiful, light *al fresco* feast.

Quail are small birds and have a tendency to dry out easily, so marinating the birds helps keep them moist. If you're using the barbecue, wrap the potatoes in foil and tuck them among the coals to roast. I've given you instructions for cooking the dish indoors as well as unfortunately the UK weather isn't always so kind to us.

The key to this dish is to keep back the quail marinade for the sauce – the fluffy potatoes soak it up like a sponge and it gives the whole dish so much extra flavour. You could try marinating duck breasts in the same way.

SERVES 4

8 quail, *160–180g each*
50g sultanas
5g smoked paprika
5g thyme
50ml extra virgin olive oil
175ml Passito di Pantelleria, Marsala or Greco di Bianco wine
2 tbsp red wine vinegar
sea salt and freshly ground black pepper

FOR THE MASHED POTATO

4 large Cyprus potatoes *(800g–1kg)*

Spatchcock the quail and put them in a large non-metallic dish or sealable container that fits all the quail in one layer.

In a bowl, mix all the remaining ingredients and pour over the quail. Cover with cling film or a lid, place in the fridge and leave to marinate overnight.

The next day, preheat the oven to 200°C/fan 180°C/gas 6. Wash the potatoes well then cut a cross in the top of each. Place on a tray and bake for 50 minutes to 1 hour, until soft. Set aside while you cook the quail – they should stay warm.

Preheat a grill on its highest setting. Lift the quail out of their marinade (reserve the marinade) and place, bone-side up, under the hot grill for 10 minutes. Turn them over and continue to grill for 15 minutes until golden. Meanwhile, reheat the reserved marinade.

To check the quail are cooked, cut along the breastbone and check there are no bloody juices (or use a thermometer pushed into the fleshy part and check it reads 75°C). Set aside to rest for 5 minutes.

Scoop the insides of the potatoes out into a bowl – they should be fluffy like mashed potato. Season with salt and pepper, then divide among warm serving plates, pile a quail on to each plate and spoon lots of the hot marinade over the top.

STUFATO DI FARAONA

GUINEA FOWL STEW WITH MUSHROOMS, CARROTS, HERBS

I GREW UP THINKING GUINEA FOWL WAS A LUXURY BIRD —
it was not that easy to come by and expensive as a result, so it was something we
butchered for a special occasion, when relatives came to visit. I love the flavour
of guinea fowl – slightly richer and gamier than chicken but not heavy at all.
Like all game it's a lean bird so cooking it this way ensures the meat is really
succulent and moist, but it can easily be adapted for chicken or even pheasant,
if you like your game.

Using ice cubes for the stock is a good trick as they will take a lot longer
to come to the boil than water does, which means the bones have more time to
release their flavour.

SERVES 6

150g carrots
150g celery sticks
500g seasonal wild mushrooms or good chestnut
    mushrooms *(cut the chestnut mushrooms
    into quarters)*
1 large guinea fowl, *about 1.5kg, jointed into 8
    (ask your butcher to do this for you and to give
    you the bones)*
8 tbsp extra virgin olive oil
200ml white wine
2kg ice cubes
130g unsmoked pancetta
100g shallots *(about 3–4), cut into 5mm dice*
1 garlic clove, *smashed with the back of a knife
    then peeled*
2 bay leaves
2 thyme sprigs
50g '00' flour
1 tbsp tomato purée
sea salt and freshly ground black pepper

Peel and trim the carrots and celery sticks, trim the end of the
mushrooms and reserve all the trimmings.

Place the guinea fowl spine and / or chicken bones into a large heavy-
bottomed saucepan with 2 tablespoons of the olive oil over a high heat
and allow them to brown all over.

Remove the bones and all the fat from the pan and add the vegetable
trimmings. Sweat for 2 – 3 minutes, until softened, then pour in half
of the wine and let it evaporate. Return the bones to the pan, add
the ice cubes, bring to the boil and then simmer, covered, for about
2 hours. Strain the stock and set aside.

Preheat the oven to 200°C / fan 180°C / gas 6.

Cut the carrot and celery into 5mm cubes and place in a large
casserole with 2 tablespoons of the olive oil, the pancetta, shallot,
garlic, bay leaves and thyme and sweat the mixture until the onions
are soft but not coloured. Transfer to a large roasting tin, around
35 × 25cm.

Heat a frying pan with 4 tablespoons of the olive oil. Season the
guinea fowl pieces with salt and pepper, dust with the flour and
fry both sides over a medium–high heat until golden brown. Lift
the guinea fowl out of the pan and into the roasting tin.

Pour the fat out of the frying pan, increase the heat to high, add the mushrooms and allow to colour, then transfer to the roasting tin. Pour the remaining wine into the pan and bring to the boil. Simmer over a high heat until reduced by half, then stir in the tomato purée. Add 1 litre of the strained stock and bring back to the boil, then pour the liquid into the roasting tin. Season well and cook in the oven for 35 minutes or until the meat is cooked through.

Any leftover stock can be frozen; it can be stored for up to 1 month and used in any recipe that calls for beef or game stock.

SALUMI

CURED MEATS

Clockwise from top left:
Calabrian *capocollo,*
ventricina, pancetta,
sopressata, capocollo
di Martina Franca,
guanciale, spicy fresh
sausage, spicy cured
sausage, *cacio spinata.*

THE TERM 'SALUMI' refers to any type of meat that has been preserved in some way – cured in salt, air-dried or smoked. Just as we preserve fish (see page 123), *salumi* was born out of a desire not to waste a precious food supply and in the case of pigs in particular, it was a good way of not letting any part of the animal go to waste. Preserving meat is a practice that is deeply ingrained in our culture and all over Italy you will find incredible different kinds of *salumi*. They fall into two categories: whole cuts, such as from the leg for prosciutto or the belly for pancetta; and ground or chopped meat that is mixed with some kind of flavouring (herbs and spices), and fat, then stuffed into a casing. Those in the casing are then divided into fresh or cured varieties.

It would be difficult to overstate the importance of the pig in the South, so most southern *salumi* is made from pork, but in the North you will also find cured wild boar, beef and even sheep. When I was growing up every family in my region made their own *salumi*. It was a big celebration and families used to gather not just for the slaughter of the pigs, but also to help in the preparation of the meat. The animals were killed in the winter, so that they could be kept cold while the meat rested for a couple of days to let the rigor mortis subside. Then the family would gather for the *provatura* – the tasting of the *salsiccia* mix (see page 55), whereby we cook a small piece of the meat and decide whether the flavour and seasoning are right. Next we prepared all the cuts for the hams, pancetta and *guanciale* before setting aside any offal

and fat. The fat was melted, sieved and set aside to solidify; any leftover was kept and used for cooking. Any offal that did not go into the *salumi* would be boiled and used in dishes such as *frittuliata* (see page 164). Finally, everything was left to hang. Generally the *salumi* were hung in the kitchen and the fire was left burning, which not only helped keep the air dry and preserve the *salumi*, but also kept the flies away. Walking past the room was a sign of luck and prosperity for the family, indicating that they would have meat for the year. Like so many artisanal skills, sadly time and economics mean that the tradition of making *salumi* at home is not as common as it was when I was growing up, but my auntie and uncle still do it. And there is nevertheless a national pride in our skills, and efforts have been made on a large scale to preserve the traditions and keep improving recipes to ensure we maintain the quality of the products and reputation we have earned as producers.

The flavour of each type of *salumi* varies widely according to the region, producer and breed of animal. If I were to generalise, I would say that northern *salumi* are characterised by a subtle, gentle flavouring, mainly using herbs. The North is also particularly renowned for excellent hams – such as the amazing *prosciutto crudo di Parma*, and *prosciutto di San Daniele*, from the Friuli region. In Calabria we are of

PRESERVING MEAT IS A PRACTICE THAT IS DEEPLY INGRAINED IN OUR CULTURE AND ALL OVER ITALY YOU WILL FIND INCREDIBLE DIFFERENT KINDS OF *SALUMI*

course famous for spicy *salumi*, especially the spreadable *n'duja*. Below is just a very brief introduction to some of the *salumi* available, focusing on some of the best from the *mezzogiorno* region and some of my favourites, but it barely scratches the surface of what's there and it's best just to get out and get tasting. Happily, *salumi* travels well, so there are some excellent Italian delicatessens around the UK, sourcing it from all over Italy.

Guanciale is similar to pancetta but with a more pronounced flavour, and while pancetta is cut from the belly, *guanciale* is taken from the pig's cheek and throat. It is more fatty than pancetta and is cured in salt and various other herbs or spices. In Puglia it will be herb-flavoured; in Sardinia, there will be a hint of myrtle; in Calabria, spicy paprika, while in Basilicata it could be a mix.

WHEN I WAS GROWING UP EVERY FAMILY IN MY REGION MADE THEIR OWN *SALUMI*

N'duja is something the Calabrians most probably inherited from the Spanish invasion – in Spain they have something very similar called *sobrasada* – but their version is smokier and not as spicy. It is largely made from parts of the pig's head (though not the cheeks, which are kept for *guanciale*), lard, liver and vast amounts of spicy red chilli, which give it its arresting red colour, before being bound up in a pig's intestine. This may not make it sound hugely appealing, which is perhaps why until recently it's not been very popular outside Calabria, but having brought it to the UK and introduced it to the Pizza Express menus, I have witnessed how people can get addicted and I'm so happy to see it appearing on menus around the country. *N'duja* is also possibly one of the most versatile *salumi*. It is very rich and it needs to be used with parsimony, so just a tablespoon is all you need to transform your stews and your tomato sauce. Lightly

coat your fish or scallops with *n'duja* and grill them, or do as we do in Calabria and spread it on bruschetta. It's like Nutella for me – I just couldn't live without it.

IN CALABRIA WE ARE OF COURSE FAMOUS FOR SPICY *SALUMI*, ESPECIALLY THE SPREADABLE *N'DUJA*

Capocollo is a whole cut taken from the upper part of the neck and part of the shoulder and is dry-cured with salt and other spices, often peppercorns. The most famous is the *capocollo di Martina Franca* from Puglia, which is cured for at least 5 months and is rich in the oaky flavour of the woods where the pigs are reared.

Ventricina is a coarse *salame* typical of Abruzzo. It's made with chopped lean pork shoulder meat, which is pressed with fat and a sweet and spicy dried chilli, paprika and fennel seeds.

Sopressata has two types, the uncured version from Toscano, and the cured one from Molise, Campania, Basilicata and Calabria. It is made from lean pork cuts mixed with fat, and the meat is hand-cut into chunks rather than ground. It is spiced with sweet red pepper, then stuffed into casings and pressed to give it its characteristic flattened shape and name. In Calabria it's considered something very refined and it's brought out on special occasions or as a mark of respect. We used to give it to our doctor when he came to the house.

Cacio spinata is another spicy Calabrian salame made with chilli and wrapped in caciocavallo cheese (see page 64 for more about the cheese). It's rich but is wonderful served as part of an antipasti or in sandwiches.

Salsiccia calabrese can be fresh and cured. Both are fiery and famous for their combination of chilli and fennel seeds. The fresh one is grilled or fried (see my recipe on page 55) and the cured one is simply sliced.

Opposite: N'duja.

CONIGLIO ALL`AGRODOLCE E LAMPASCIONI

SWEET AND SOUR RABBIT WITH PICKLED LAMPASCIONI

SULTANAS, SUGAR AND SWEATED SHALLOTS add the sweetness, while a healthy dose of vinegar and pickled *lampascioni* provide the sour in this simple dish, a reflection of the *mezzogiorno's* Moorish heritage.

Puglians love to pickle and their *lampascioni* (hyacinth bulbs, see page 193), with their delicate sweet and bitter flavours, are a perfect candidate. You can buy pickled *lampascioni* online from one of the stockists listed on page 286, but if you'd like something easier to track down use pickled *borettane* onions, which are widely available in supermarkets – they'll give the dish the bitterness it needs. I'm going to gently encourage you to keep the offal, for the extra texture and flavour it provides but if offal really isn't your thing, then do just leave it out.

SERVES 4

3 tbsp extra virgin olive oil
1.8kg rabbit, *jointed into 8 pieces (ask your butcher to do this for you and to give you the liver, heart and kidneys)*
50g '00' flour
1 celery stick, *finely diced*
½ fennel bulb, *trimmed and finely diced*
½ onion, *finely diced*
75g shallots (*about 1–2*), *finely diced*
1 garlic clove, *finely chopped*
80g carrots, *peeled and finely diced*
30g sun-dried tomatoes, *finely diced*
½ tsp fennel seeds
500ml red wine vinegar
50g molasses sugar
2 tbsp tomato purée
1 litre chicken stock
100g pickled lampascioni, Borretane or other wild onions
75g small black pitted olives
40g sultanas
1 marjoram sprig, *chopped*
1 thyme sprig, *leaves only, chopped*
25g pistachio nuts, *chopped*
30g pine nuts, *toasted*
sea salt and freshly ground black pepper

Preheat the oven to 180°C / fan 160°C / gas 4.

Heat 2 tablespoons of the olive oil in a large casserole over a medium heat, dust the rabbit with the flour, then add to the casserole and cook, stirring frequently, for about 8–10 minutes, until evenly browned. Remove with a slotted spoon and set aside

Add the celery, fennel, onion, shallot, garlic, carrot, sun-dried tomato and fennel seeds to the casserole, stir well, cover and cook over a low heat for about 5 minutes, until the onions are starting to soften. Stir in the vinegar, sugar and tomato purée and simmer, stirring occasionally, until reduced to a thick paste.

Return the rabbit pieces to the casserole, pour in the stock then transfer to the oven. Bake for 20 minutes. Add the pickled wild onions, olives, sultanas, marjoram and thyme and season to taste with salt and pepper. Bake for a further 15–20 minutes, until the rabbit is cooked through.

Heat a small frying pan with the remaining tablespoon of olive oil over a high heat and fry the liver, heart and kidneys for a few seconds on each side, until golden brown. Arrange the rabbit pieces and offal in a serving dish, pour the sauce over the top and garnish with the pistachios and toasted pine nuts.

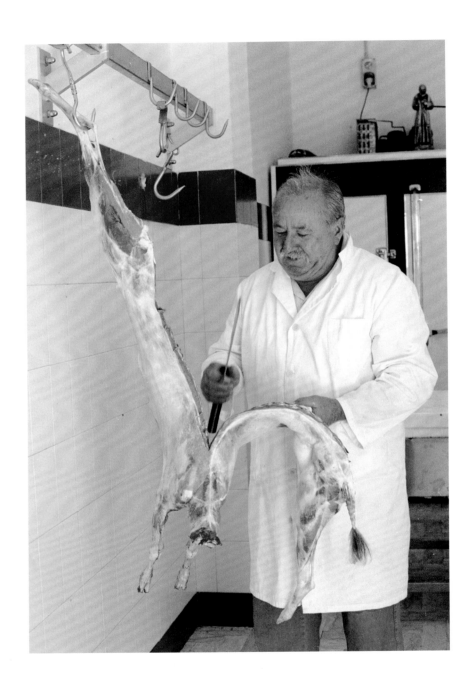

SPALLA DI AGNELLO FORNARINA

GRATIN OF SLOW-COOKED LAMB SHOULDER

FORNARINA IS THE FEMININE WORD FOR 'BREADMAKER', but really it refers to any woman who cooks using a wood-fired oven, which, throughout my childhood, was many of the women in my town. In many southern households, a wood-fired oven was just part of the armoury at a household's disposal, and a *fornarina* grew up being taught the secrets of the oven from her mother or grandmother. She understands the oven and its rhythm; how to control the temperature but also how to use it thriftily. Over 24 hours she knows which is the best time to roast peppers or aubergines, when to cook the pizza, bake the bread or use the ashes to slowly cook large cuts of meat. Then at night, when the oven is still warm, she will leave figs, black olives and tomatoes inside to dry them out in its residual heat. I've often marvelled at the *fornarina's* skill.

This lamb would traditionally have been cooked in the wood-fired oven very, very slowly over many hours. I've speeded up that process by simmering the lamb in stock and wine to add flavour, then finishing it in the oven and under the grill to brown the crust and to try and mimic the effects of the smoky wood-fired oven. You might think it's unusual to use rosé wine to cook meat, but I find red too strong; it can overpower the sweetness of the lamb. Rosé is milder and produces a nice light-coloured gravy.

SERVES 4

100ml extra virgin olive oil
2kg lamb shoulder, *with bone*
2 litres chicken stock
750ml rosé wine
4 cloves
2 bay leaves
6 juniper berries
½ tsp tomato purée
900g Cyprus or King Edward potatoes, *peeled and cut into chunks*
600g carrots, *peeled and cut into chunks*
1 garlic bulb, *top sliced off*
sea salt and freshly ground black pepper

Heat 2 tablespoons of the olive oil in a large roasting tin. Season the lamb shoulder with salt and pepper and fry it in the oil over a high heat, until nicely seared all over.

Drain the fat from the tin, pour in the chicken stock and rosé wine, then add the cloves, bay leaves, juniper berries and tomato purée. Cover with foil, bring to the boil, then lower the heat and simmer for about 1½ hours. Skim the fat from the surface from time to time and reserve. Remove the shoulder from the stock and keep on the side.

Preheat the oven to 170°C/fan 150°C/gas 3.

Bring the stock back to the boil and bubble to reduce it by half.

Place the shoulder back in the reduced stock. Add the potato, carrot and the garlic head, then transfer to the oven and cook for about 1 hour, occasionally basting the top of the meat with the juices in the pan until the lamb is tender and cooked through.

continued overleaf

FOR THE CRUST
100g fresh breadcrumbs
25g parsley
15g mint
6 marjoram sprigs
50g pecorino cheese, *finely grated*
50ml extra virgin olive oil
2 tbsp white wine

Remove the tin from the oven and pour the stock into a saucepan (leave the lamb and vegetables in the roasting tin). Add the garlic cloves to the stock by squeezing the skins of the roasted bulb and reduce the stock until thickened – it should be like a light gravy – and very aromatic. Increase the oven setting to 210°C / fan 190°C / gas 7.

While the stock is reducing, use your hands to mix all the crust ingredients until well combined. Spread over the lamb shoulder and place it back in the oven with the vegetables for 10 minutes then place under a hot grill for a few minutes to brown the crust.

To serve, slice the meat. Spoon the vegetables on to warm serving plates, top with lamb slices and pour the gravy around the plate (not over the crust otherwise it won't be crispy!).

FRISSURATA DI POLLO RUSPANTE

FRIED CHICKEN PIECES

THE ITALIAN NAME OF THIS DISH comes from the pan that it was traditionally cooked in – a *frissura* is a wide cast-iron pan usually used on an open fire. The best English description for the dish is somewhat less romantic; it's probably best conveyed to you as 'fried chicken and chips'. Thin potato wedges are roasted on top of the chicken so they soak up all its cooking juices as well as the flavour from the pancetta. The result is seriously good chips.

Cooking chicken on an open flame in the big heavy pan was difficult as you had less control than you do on a modern hob. The cook had to be skilled so that they didn't fry and brown the outside of the chicken before the middle was cooked. In the same way, to be successful with this dish the chicken pieces need to be small otherwise they won't cook through. I've used a jointed chicken because my culture has instilled me with a need to use as much of an animal as I can, but you could make things simpler and use halved chicken thighs. Whichever route you choose, it's really important to cut the chicken pieces in half – you'll need a meat cleaver or machete to do this, or ask your butcher to do it for you.

SERVES 6

180g unsmoked pancetta, *diced*

1.5kg chicken, *jointed into 8, each piece cut in half (ask your butcher to do this for you) or use 8 chicken thighs, cut in half*

1 garlic bulb, *peeled and cloves separated*

10g sage, *leaves picked*

10g rosemary, *roughly chopped*

100ml white wine

800g Cyprus potatoes, *peeled and cut into finger-sized wedges*

150ml hot chicken stock

10g flat-leaf parsley, *roughly chopped*

5g marjoram, *roughly chopped*

sea salt and freshly ground black pepper

Preheat the oven to 200°C / fan 180°C / gas 6.

Heat a large frying pan over a medium–high heat until hot, then add the pancetta and fry until it releases its fat. Push the pancetta to the side of the pan and add 3–4 chicken pieces. Cook on each side until golden brown, then transfer to a large roasting tin (about 35 × 25cm), scraping in the browned pancetta at the same time.

Continue to brown the chicken pieces in batches until all of them are done. Add the garlic and herbs to the pan and cook for a couple of minutes until starting to soften and golden. Pour away and discard any excess fat in the pan. Add the wine and allow the alcohol to evaporate.

Meanwhile, blanch the potatoes in a large pan of salted boiling water for 1 minute, then drain and transfer to a bowl. Season with salt and pepper. Lay the potatoes on top of the chicken, pour in the stock and bake for around 40 minutes until the chicken and potatoes are cooked.

Lift out the potatoes and chicken and transfer to a warm serving dish. Stir the chopped parsley and marjoram into the sauce left in the roasting tin, then pour over the chicken.

Clockwise from top left:
Sweet chilli paste, dried
chillies, *pipi cruschi*,
Thai-style red chillies,
chopped fresh chillies
preserved in olive oil,
spicy paprika.

PEPERONCINI

CHILLIES

ONE OF THE MOST BEAUTIFUL SIGHTS of the summer in South Italy is the bright red chains of chilli peppers, strung together and hung from every balcony, roof top and windowsill around the region, particularly in Calabria and Basilicata. People are often surprised to discover that chillies are used a lot in southern Italian cooking; spice is not something that's generally associated with Italian food, but in certain regions chilli is an important part of our culture – fresh, dried, ground into a powder, as a paste – it runs all the way through our cooking. In some households it's like salt and you'll always find a selection of fresh or dried chillies on the table at mealtimes, just as you would salt and pepper mills in other houses. We use it as a condiment, in *salumi*, with fish, with pasta, even in desserts.

Calabria has the spiciest food in Italy, and a long and passionate association with the chilli. When you say something is '*calabrese*' you're automatically expecting something fiery.

IN SOME HOUSEHOLDS CHILLI IS LIKE SALT AND YOU'LL ALWAYS FIND A SELECTION ON THE TABLE AT MEALTIMES

Basilicata is also a big consumer of chillies but there they are generally milder. One of Basilicata's most well-known chillies is *pipi cruschi*, a dried sweet chilli. The traditional way to cook them is to fry the whole chilli in very hot olive oil for just 2 or 3 seconds and they become like crisps. We eat them as a snack with a glass of wine, crumbled over fried eggs for breakfast or on top of a *linguine aglio olio* (see page 87).

Given its importance to our cuisine, it's surprising that nowhere in southern Italy has an indigenous variety of chilli. Christopher Columbus brought *capsicum annuum* (chilli pepper) seeds to Europe from Central and South America and the varieties he brought, along with many other Asian varieties, are the ones we continue to grow today. However, like any fruit or vegetable, grown in our soil, using our water, our sun and our passion, the South Italian chillies have their own distinctive flavours (and degrees of spiciness). And work is being done in Calabria to change the status that the chilli holds. The *Academia Italiana del Peperoncino* (Chilli Academy), founded in 1994 by the journalist Enzo Monaco (we're pictured together on page 145), was created to spread

THE *ACADEMIA ITALIANA DEL PEPERONCINO* WAS CREATED TO SPREAD 'SPICY CULTURE' IN ITALY

'spicy culture' in Italy and most importantly to promote research into the production and growing of chillies. It has been campaigning to have the *peperoncino Calabrese* granted PGI (Protected Geographic Indication) status to recognise the value and quality of the chillies we grow – sadly at the time of writing it has not yet been successful.

The Academy also organises an internationally acclaimed chilli festival every September in the Calabrian coastal town of Diamante. It's a celebration of the small fiery fruit, with workshops, tastings, talks from international experts, and a chilli-eating contest where participants are given a 500g bowl of hot chillies and compete to see who can eat the most in the least time. I've been several times and it's a fun, festive occasion where the sense of pride in our regional product is palpable.

A chilli's spiciness depends on the amount of capsaicin held in the seeds. It's thought to be what makes chilli good for our hearts, but it's also what makes the fruit slightly addictive. The more chilli you eat, the more your tastebuds get used to the heat, the more your body gets used to the pleasure–pain experience that comes from eating something spicy and the more heat you will want until eventually you're no longer able to taste other flavours. Chefs have to be particularly careful with tasting chilli, so that we don't ruin our palates.

The best introduction to Calabrian chilli is through our *salumi*, so if I haven't yet convinced you, I can only urge you again to try our *salsiccia Calabrese* and our *n'duja*, but if you want a slightly gentler introduction then try my recipe for chilli jam (see page 274), and serve it drizzled over burrata, mozzarella or as a dip for fried squid or deep-fried courgette flowers (see page 202).

A CHILLI'S SPICINESS DEPENDS ON THE AMOUNT OF CAPSAICIN HELD IN THE SEEDS – IT'S WHAT MAKES THE FRUIT SLIGHTLY ADDICTIVE

PANCIA DI MAIALE NERO STRACOTTA E SANGUINACCIO

SLOW-COOKED PORK BELLY WITH PIG'S BLOOD

YOU WON'T FIND SANGUINACCIO ON MENUS in any Italian restaurants these days – health and safety forbid it – but you will still find sweet puddings made from its key ingredient – fresh pig's blood – in homes around Italy. It's traditionally made around the time the pigs are slaughtered, in the winter, and for me, it has strong childhood associations as my grandmother often used to give it to us, calling it 'Nutella' to try and make us eat it. Chocolate, milk, pine nuts, cinnamon, bread or candied orange or lemon can be mixed with the blood, depending on regional preferences, and honestly, despite its richness, if you didn't know what you were eating, you wouldn't necessarily guess! Here I've adapted the principle of the pudding to make a sweet sauce for the deeply savoury pork belly. Black pudding replaces the blood, and I've stirred in *mostarda di frutta* (quite a northern addition usually), which adds a bit of spiciness as well as sweetness. The sauce should be thick enough that it's almost spreadable.

SERVES 6

½ tsp fennel seeds
5 juniper berries
2 bay leaves
2 tsp fine sea salt
1.5kg skinless pork belly, *with bone*
juice of ½ lemon

FOR THE PIG'S BLOOD SAUCE
250g black pudding sausage
2½ tbsp clear honey
25g mostarda di frutta or good-quality candied fruit
grated zest of 1 orange plus 50ml orange juice
grated zest of 1 lemon plus 50ml lemon juice
20g blanched almonds, *roughly chopped*
ground black pepper

Preheat the oven to 140°C / fan 120°C / gas 1.

Using a pestle and mortar, crush the fennel seeds, juniper berries and bay leaf with the salt. Pat the spices on to the flesh side of the pork only. Set aside for 10 minutes.

Put a roasting tray or pan full of water at the bottom of the oven so that it will create some steam and keep the meat moist. Brush off the spiced rub and put the belly in another oven tray and cook for 1 hour, then remove the pan with the water and cook for another 3 hours. Remove the meat from the oven and allow to rest for 30 minutes.

While the pork is resting, make the sauce. Put all the ingredients into a food processor or blender and process until you have a smooth sauce. Put into a saucepan, season with black pepper and heat gently.

Trim the meat and cut out the bone, then cut the belly crossways into 3cm strips.

Heat a frying pan over a high heat. Put a sheet of baking parchment in the bottom of the pan and sear the belly on all four sides. Transfer to a warm serving dish and squeeze over the lemon juice. Serve with the warm sauce alongside.

COSTINE DI AGNELLO E CARCIOFI

LAMB CUTLETS WITH ARTICHOKES

MORE ARTICHOKES, I CAN HEAR YOU SAY, but they're such a fantastic vegetable, and so underused in the UK that I want to try and persuade you to cook with them more. Although this is something we'd often cook for Easter Day or Easter Monday, using the best of the spring lamb, it's actually such an easy dish to prepare and once you've mastered your artichoke prep, I guarantee you it could become an addition to your mid-week repertoire. It's also a really forgiving, adaptable recipe so swap the artichokes for red peppers if you want a change, and scale the quantities up or down to cater for fewer or a party.

SERVES 4

juice of 1 lemon
4 artichokes, *preferably mammole or violet (don't use globe)*
2 tbsp olive oil
12 lamb cutlets
3 large Cyprus potatoes, *peeled and cut into wedges*
1 garlic clove, *smashed with the back of a knife*
125ml white wine
400ml hot chicken or vegetable stock
1 tsp dried oregano
sea salt and freshly ground black pepper

Preheat the oven to 210°C/fan 190°C/gas 7.

Start by preparing the artichokes. Mix the lemon juice into a bowl of cold water. Clean each artichoke one at a time by picking off the external leaves until you reach the tender ones. Scoop out the hairy choke with a spoon (discard it) and peel the tough skin from the stalk. Cut the artichoke in half and then into quarters. Place in the bowl of acidulated water to prevent discolouring. Repeat with the remaining artichokes.

Heat 1 tablespoon of the oil in a large frying pan and pan-fry the lamb cutlets in batches, three to four at a time, until seared and golden on each side. Transfer to a large roasting tin and spread out in a single layer (keep the frying pan of rendered fat to one side).

Place the potato wedges in a large pan of boiling salted water. Bring back to the boil and drain immediately.

Drain the artichokes and add to the roasting tin, then spoon the potatoes all around. Everything should sit in an even layer – more or less.

Drain the fat from the frying pan then put over a medium heat. Add the garlic clove to the pan and fry for 1–2 minutes, until golden. Pour in the wine and bring to a simmer. Allow the wine to evaporate, then add the stock and bring to the boil. Pour this liquid into the tin. Season well with salt and pepper and drizzle over a tablespoon of olive oil.

Bake in the oven for 35 minutes, until the cutlets are cooked through. Remove from the oven, sprinkle over the oregano and leave to rest for 5–10 minutes before serving.

FRITTULIATA

STEAMED PIG'S OFFAL WITH CABBAGE

WHEN PEOPLE THINK ABOUT ITALIAN FOOD, they tend to think about the colourful vegetables, the olive oils and the bright, fresh pasta dishes. That is of course a huge part of it, but beyond the vegetables, so much rural cuisine is based on cooking with what's available, and for many households that means stretching ingredients and using the land around them to grow their food or raise a few livestock. The *cucina povera* of the *mezzogiorno* region is rooted in the principle that we don't waste a thing, so nose-to-tail eating is a strong part of our culture, and no dish is more emblematic of it than this one. There are so many ways to serve this dish. I love to serve it as a snack to accompany drinks – you just put the dish on the table and leave everyone to help themselves, wrapping bits of the meat in a cabbage leaf or nibbling on the pickles. But you could serve it as a main course for four. It's rich so don't leave out the pickles – you need the acidity to cut through the richness. I'm also aware that not everyone loves offal like we do, so if you're not quite up to eating tails, ears or tongues, just use the belly, trotters and any other pieces you feel up to trying.

The recipe makes more stock than you need (you'll be left with about 2.5 litres), but it freezes well and would be great as the basis of any soup dish.

SERVES 4 AS A MAIN COURSE

FOR THE COOKING LIQUID
6 litres water
1 litre white wine
100ml white wine vinegar
3 bay leaves
8 juniper berries
8 cloves
2 tbsp salt

FOR THE PORK
400g pork belly, *skin on*
2 pig's tails
2 pig's ears
2 pig's cheeks
2 pig's snouts
2 pig's trotters
2 pig's tongues
2 pig's ribs

Put all the ingredients for the cooking liquid into a very large pot (or divide it between 2 large pots or saucepans), making sure there's enough room to add all the cuts of the pig. Cover with a lid and bring to the boil.

Add the pork belly, tail, ears, cheeks, snout and trotters and simmer on a medium heat for about 1½ hours, covered with a lid. At this point add the tongue and the ribs and cook for 1 hour more.

In the meantime, peel the potatoes and carrots, cutting the potatoes into quarters and the carrots in half if they're very large. Cut the leeks into 7–8 cm lengths and separate the cabbage leaves.

About 15–20 minutes before the meat is cooked, add all the vegetables. When all the pig cuts are tender, remove the pan from the hob. Lift the meat and vegetables out of the liquid into a bowl and set aside to cool. Pass the cooking liquid through a sieve and cool then chill overnight. When it's completely cold carefully skim the fat from the top of the set stock.

FOR THE VEGETABLES

600g King Edward potatoes
350g carrots
2 leeks, *trimmed*
6–8 Savoy cabbage leaves

TO SERVE

Pickled vegetable salad *(see page 191)*

When ready to eat, put the meat and vegetables back into the large pan and cover with just enough stock. Cover with a lid and gently bring to the boil until everything has heated through. Serve with the pickled vegetables.

INVOLTINI DI PODOLICA, CACIOCAVALLO E FUNGHI SELVATICI

BEEF ROLLED WITH CHEESE AND WILD MUSHROOMS

WE DON'T HAVE A BIG CULTURE OF COOKING BEEF in the South. Buffalo are bred for mozzarella, but cattle has historically been a working animal. We used our cattle in the fields, so beef cattle were expensive and too much of the animal was wasted to make it a rewarding investment. As the South has shed its economic shackles that is changing and the culture of using beef is growing. That said, *involtini* use the animal in a way that is in keeping with our culture of stretching meat to make it go further. Small quantities of beef are bashed until very thin, then rolled around a filling.

In Italy I would use beef from Podolica cows, which are bred in the Sila mountains. It's a beautiful place where the cows graze outdoors all year round and the grass is iron-rich. The meat is lean, which means it is tougher, so you need to beat and rest it – to tenderise it before cooking and watch it carefully during the cooking to ensure it doesn't dry out. In the UK, medallions are likely to come from grain-fed beef fillet and be fattier and more tender, which will ensure they remain moist.

Serve these *involtini* with a nice glass of Cirò wine and the dandelion greens with breadcrumbs (see page 180).

SERVES 4

800g beef medallions *(about 60–70g each)*
6 tbsp extra virgin olive oil
1 garlic clove, *skin on, halved*
1 rosemary sprig
1 thyme sprig
400g mixed wild mushrooms, *trimmed*
10g flat-leaf parsley, *finely chopped*
10g chives, *finely chopped*
10g marjoram, *finely chopped*
50g mozzarella cheese, *torn*
60g pecorino cheese, *grated*
250g caciocavallo cheese or young, soft pecorino
   cheese or smoked or unsmoked scamorza, *crumbled*

Place the beef medallions between two sheets of cling film and bash them with a rolling pin until they are each 5mm thick, then set aside.

In a pan heat 2 tablespoons of the olive oil over a medium heat with the garlic, rosemary and thyme. Add the mushrooms, season with salt and pepper, and fry for a couple of minutes on a very high heat (be careful not to burn the garlic – remove it if necessary) until the mushrooms are browned and soft.

Let the mushrooms cool completely, then roughly chop two-thirds of them and place in a bowl. Add the herbs, mozzarella, grated pecorino and caciocavallo cheeses and mix well.

Put about a tablespoon of the mixture on the shorter ends of each slice of beef and roll up, being careful to enclose the ends of the rolls as you roll by tucking the sides in. Secure each roll with two rosemary sprigs or toothpicks.

continued overleaf

30g '00' flour
200ml white wine
300ml chicken stock
5g parsley leaves, roughly chopped
sea salt and freshly ground black pepper

*You will also need some rosemary sprigs
or toothpicks to secure the rolls*

Preheat the oven to 200°C/fan 180°C/gas 6.

Season the rolls with salt and pepper and dust them with the flour. Heat the remaining 4 tablespoons of olive oil in a large frying pan over a medium–high heat and add the rolls. Fry until seared and sealed all over, then pour in the white wine and allow it to evaporate. Add the reserved mushrooms and the chicken stock, then transfer to a large baking dish and place in the oven for 7–8 minutes. Check they are hot right through by sticking a toothpick into the centre of a couple of rolls; it should come out warm.

Lift the rolls out of the sauce into a serving dish and remove the rosemary or toothpicks. stir the parsley into the sauce and pour over the rolls.

FILETTO DI CINGHIALE LIQUIRIZIA E BERGAMOTTO

WILD BOAR MARINATED IN LIQUORICE AND BERGAMOT ZEST

LIQUORICE WORKS WELL WITH GAME as it has the power to match up to the strong flavour of the meat. I've used liquorice powder here as opposed to the liqueur or the sticks as the powder has the most sweetness. Whichever you choose, complement the iron-rich meat with something bitter and tangy, such as the turnip tops with bottarga (see page 178) or the dandelion greens with breadcrumbs (see page 180). The marinade works just as well with duck, venison, pheasant or hare.

SERVES 4

2 wild boar or venison fillets *(about 500–600g in total)*
about 300ml extra virgin olive oil
grated zest of ½ bergamot or 1 orange
juice of 1 orange
½ tsp liquorice powder
pinch of black fennel seeds
1 banana shallot, *roughly chopped*
6 juniper berries, *lightly crushed*
4 cloves
1 bay leaf
1 garlic clove, *unpeeled and smashed with the back of a knife*
10g rosemary, *roughly chopped*
10g sage, *roughly chopped*
1 dried red chilli, *crushed*
sea salt and freshly ground black pepper

Put the wild boar fillets into a large sealable container so they lie in an even layer. Mix all the remaining ingredients together in a bowl and pour over the boar, then cover with the lid and transfer to the fridge. Leave to marinate overnight.

The next day, heat the oven to 210°C / fan 190°C / gas 7.

Heat a frying pan until smoking hot. Lift the fillets out of the marinade and drain well, keeping the marinade to one side. Season the fillets with salt and sear each side in the hot pan until sealed and golden brown. Brush with the marinade then transfer to an oven tray and bake in the oven for 15–18 minutes – it should still be pink in the middle. Transfer the meat to a board, cover with foil and allow to rest for 5–10 minutes.

Drain any pink juices from the rested boar and pour into the roasting tin. Swirl the tin around with the other juices already in there. The heat of the pan will cook any bloody juices.

Slice the fillet and divide among four warm plates, then drizzle a spoonful of the juices over the top.

INVOLTINI DI FEGATO E RETINA

LIVER ROLLS STUFFED WITH PANCETTA AND TURNIP TOPS

TRADITIONALLY, the liver used in this dish would of course have been pig's liver. The liver was the first thing you'd eat after you killed the pig as it's the only organ that isn't stressed after the kill so it stays soft and moist when cooked. Here, I've used calves' liver, which is slightly more refined, and much more readily available in the UK. While calves' livers are naturally more tender than pigs', this also means they can dry out more easily, which is why I've wrapped the *involtini* in caul fat or pancetta before frying them.

SERVES 4

1 garlic clove, *finely chopped*
1 sage sprig, *finely chopped*
2 rosemary sprigs, *finely chopped*
60g unsmoked pancetta
200g caul fat, *cut into four 20 × 10cm pieces,*
    or 200g unsmoked pancetta slices
4 × 100–125g thin slices of calves' liver
1–2 tbsp extra virgin olive oil

FOR THE SALMORIGLIO SAUCE

½ garlic clove, *halved*
1 thyme sprig
½ tsp dried oregano
1 bay leaf
50ml olive oil
25ml red wine vinegar

FOR THE CIME DI RAPA

500g cime di rapa (turnip tops)
2 tbsp olive oil
½ red chilli, *roughly chopped*
½ garlic clove, *smashed with the back of a knife*

Start by preparing the salmoriglio sauce. Put the garlic, thyme, oregano and bay leaf into a bowl, then stir in the oil and vinegar. Cover and set aside overnight.

The next day, preheat the oven to 210°C/fan 190°C/gas 7. Place the cime di rapa in a bowl of iced water.

Mix the garlic, sage, rosemary and pancetta until thoroughly combined. Place a piece of caul fat on a board so it's lying flat or lay out enough pancetta slices to make roughly a 20 × 10cm rectangle. Put a slice of liver on top then spoon a quarter of the seasoned pancetta stuffing into the middle. Roll up the liver, wrapping the caul fat or pancetta tightly around it, and smoothing it down at the end. Repeat with the remaining caul or pancetta, liver and stuffing.

Brush the oil over each parcel. Heat a frying pan over a very high heat. Place two of the liver parcels in the pan with the join underneath. This is very important otherwise the parcels can come undone. Fry for 1–2 minutes, turning them on to each side until they're golden all over. Transfer to a roasting tin and cook in the oven for 6–8 minutes – the filling will be piping hot.

Strain the salmoriglio sauce through a sieve and into a bowl and set aside.

Bring a large pan of salted water to the boil and drain the cime di rapa. Blanch the cime di rapa in the pan of salted water for 3 minutes, then drain and put straight into a fresh bowl of iced water.

Heat the olive oil in a large saucepan and add the chilli and garlic. Cook over a medium heat until soft, then add the cime di rapa and fry for 2–3 minutes until coloured. Lift out of the pan and drain on kitchen paper.

Divide the cime di rapa between serving plates, place the involtini on top, then drizzle over the salmoriglio sauce.

5
VEGETALI

CIME DI RAPA E BOTTARGA

TURNIP TOPS WITH BOTTARGA

TRANSLATED AS TURNIP TOPS, *cime di rapa* are a bitter green, in season from September to January. The name is deceptive, however. *Cime di rapa* are from the turnip family but are more closely related to broccoli, and broccoli is often used as a substitute in recipes when turnip tops aren't in season. *Cime di rapa* are at their best in October, when the leaves are the youngest and most tender and if you buy them at this time you should be able to use the whole head. However, as the season progresses the leaves will get hardier and you will need to remove the very tough outer ones. They are a very popular vegetable in the South and the most common way to prepare them is with garlic, chilli and anchovies. I've replaced the anchovies with bottarga here. The greens have quite a strong flavour so bottarga gives the dish the same gentle salty backnote without fighting the flavour of the turnip tops so it's perfectly balanced. Serve with steamed fish or grilled prawns.

SERVES 4

1kg cime di rapa (turnip tops)
1 tbsp olive oil
1 garlic clove, *finely sliced*
1 red chilli, *finely sliced*
50g bottarga (dried mullet roe)
sea salt

Clean the turnip tops, discard the very hard outer leaves, trim off the base of the stems and place in iced water for about 20 minutes.

Bring a pan of salted water to the boil and blanch the turnip tops for about 2 minutes – this will remove some of the bitterness but keep them nice and crunchy. Drain well and gently squeeze the greens with your hands to remove excess water.

Heat the olive oil in a frying pan over a medium heat and fry the garlic and chilli until the garlic is starting to turn golden (do not allow it to burn). Remove the garlic slices from the pan and add the turnip tops to the chilli. Toss over a high heat to sear and colour the tops, then take the pan off the heat. Return the garlic to the pan and toss it through. Season with salt, if necessary, then transfer to a serving dish and finish by grating over the bottarga.

CIPOLLA DI TROPEA ALL' INSALATA

CARAMELISED TROPEA ONION SALAD

ONIONS ARE NATURALLY SWEET and cooking them very slowly will cause their natural sugars to caramelise, but adding a hint of icing sugar speeds up the process and gives them a little bit of crunch too. This is an unusual dish, which is a fantastic starter or a good accompaniment to oily fish, such as mackerel or sardines, as the mild acidity in the onions and the salty olives cut through their richness.

SERVES 4

600g red Tropea onions (or griotte, sweet white or Roscoff onions), *peeled and halved lengthways*
1 tbsp icing sugar
1 tbsp extra virgin olive oil
1–2 tbsp Red Onion Jam *(see page 277)*
100g pitted Italian black olives
15g pine nuts, *toasted*
8g chives, *roughly chopped*
1 tsp black sesame seeds

FOR THE DRESSING
2 tsp mosto cotto (grape must syrup) or balsamic syrup
2 tsp red wine vinegar
4 tsp extra virgin olive oil
pinch of sea salt

Place the onions cut-side up on a board and dust with the icing sugar. Leave to one side until the sugar has melted.

Heat the oil in a non-stick frying pan over a medium–high heat. Add the onions, cut-side down, cover with a lid or plate a bit smaller than the size of the pan to press the onions down and cook until the sugar has caramelised and the onions are golden. Remove from the heat and leave the onions in the pan for about 10 minutes.

Meanwhile, in a bowl whisk the ingredients for the dressing and put to one side.

Separate the onion leaves, transfer to a serving dish and toss with the dressing. Scatter over the black olives and dot the onion jam around the plate. Scatter over the pine nuts, chives and black sesame seeds.

CICORIA E MOLLICA SALTATA

DANDELION GREENS WITH BREADCRUMBS

CICORIA TARASSACO, best translated as dandelion greens (very different to the yellow flowers!), is a bitter green leaf from the chicory family, in season from around November to February. The greens are quite difficult to get hold of in the UK but you can substitute another bitter leaf, such as puntarelle or leafy chicory (not the pale Belgian endive). Soaking the dandelion is an important step because it will keep the leaves green and shiny and give them a slight bite even after cooking; it also removes some of the bitterness.

SERVES 4

300g dandelion greens (or other bitter green leaves, such as puntarelle or leafy chicory)
3 tbsp extra virgin olive oil
2 garlic cloves, *with skin, halved*
2 dried chillies, *roughly chopped*
50g fresh breadcrumbs
sea salt

Separate the leaves, discard any tough outer leaves and trim the bottom of the stems. Soak the leaves in iced water for 1 hour – this will help to remove some of the bitterness and will cause them to curl.

Heat two tablespoons of the olive oil over a medium heat and sweat the garlic until it is just starting to turn golden. Add the chilli, then the breadcrumbs, tossing them in the oil until the breadcrumbs turn crisp – about 3–4 minutes – then remove to a bowl.

Meanwhile, bring a pan of salted water to the boil and blanch the leaves for 5 minutes.

Add the remaining tablespoon of oil to the frying pan and place on a medium heat. Drain the cooked greens and once cool enough to handle gently squeeze out the excess water using your hands. Add to the pan and toss and fry until the greens starts to colour. Remove and add to the bowl of breadcrumbs. Mix well before serving.

CIAMBOTTA DI VERDURE

PAN-FRIED VEGETABLES SERVED IN BREAD

PAN-FRIED MEDITERRANEAN VEGETABLES with scrambled eggs stuffed inside a loaf is the best way to describe this dish, but really that is underselling it as *ciambotta* is one of my favourite recipes in the book, completely addictive and a real crowd-pleaser. When I was growing up Mum used to make it the night before a visit to the Madonna. On Sunday mornings my parents used to march us all up the hill behind our house to pay our respects and this was our mid-morning snack: huge fat wedges of juicy, eggy vegetable bread. Looking at the picture opposite, you'd be right to think that for most people, a hefty slice of this would be more than enough for a meal, but of course, we'd climb back down the hill for a big Sunday lunch later. At home, we'd stuff this into a huge Cerchiara loaf (see page 256), which would give us lunches, snacks and dinners for days, but if you're not going to embark on making one, the quantity here will fill the specified weight of sourdough and give a family a hearty meal or two at least. The flavours keep maturing so that it just gets better and better, and the juices inside the bread keep it moist so it won't go stale. Alternatively you could halve the recipe and use a 1.25kg sourdough loaf.

SERVES 12

4 tbsp extra virgin olive oil, *plus extra to drizzle*
600g red peppers, *cut into 1.5cm cubes*
320g courgette, *cut into 1.5cm cubes*
350g aubergine, *cut into 1.5cm cubes*
300g red onions, *cut into 1.5cm cubes*
1 × 2.5kg sourdough loaf, *or 2 × 1.25kg loaves*
4 medium eggs, *lightly beaten*
10g flat-leaf parsley, *roughly chopped*
10g basil, *roughly chopped*
pinch of dried oregano
30g pecorino cheese, *grated*
sea salt and freshly ground black pepper

Heat a tablespoon of the olive oil in a large sauté pan and cook the red pepper over a medium heat until softened and lightly coloured, seasoning with salt and pepper, then transfer to a large bowl. Add another tablespoon of oil to the pan and fry the courgette in the same way then remove and add to the bowl of pepper. Repeat with the aubergine and red onion.

Cut a circle off the top of the bread, about a quarter of the way down, and tear out almost all the insides to make something similar to a pot.

Mix the vegetables together, stir the eggs into the hot vegetables and season with the fresh herbs, oregano and the cheese. Check the seasoning and pile the mixture into the bread shell.

Drizzle with olive oil, cover with the bread's top, and leave to firm up overnight at room temperature, flipping the bread three or four times, so that it becomes evenly soaked in all the oil and vegetable juices. Serve cut into wedges.

CAPONATA
DI MELANZANE

SWEET AND SOUR AUBERGINE

ANOTHER OF SICILY'S FAMOUS CULINARY EXPORTS, and undoubtedly a favourite on the island, the mixture of sweet and sour vegetables has as many interpretations as cooks. The classic recipe takes the best of the abundance of the island's summer bounty – aubergines, courgettes, peppers, fennel, tomatoes, basil – and reduces them to a rich, sweet and sour stew with olives, pine nuts and sultanas, but the basic notion can be carried over into the winter too with the season's root vegetables, among others, or as I've done here, limited to just one – aubergines. Eat *caponata* warm or at room temperature. Serve it alongside lamb or other grilled meats, with mozzarella or burrata, or just pile it high on to bruschetta. The flavours get better and better the longer you leave it.

SERVES 4 — 6

about 1.5 litres sunflower oil, *for deep-frying*
1kg purple aubergines, *cut into 2cm cubes*
100g celery, *cut into 2cm pieces*
250ml red wine vinegar
20g tomato purée
2 tbsp clear honey
1 tbsp dark brown sugar
50ml extra virgin olive oil, plus an extra tbsp
20g mint leaves
800g pitted green olives *(I use Castelvetrano)*
½ tsp dried oregano
20g sultanas, *soaked in water overnight*
2 garlic cloves, *sliced*
20g pine nuts

Heat the sunflower oil in a deep saucepan – it should come about a third or halfway up the sides.

Once the oil reaches 180°C, deep-fry the aubergine in batches – it's important to do it in batches so that the aubergine doesn't crowd the pan and cause the temperature to drop or you'll have soggy aubergine. Drain on kitchen paper.

Blanch the celery in salted boiling water for 20 seconds, then drain and transfer to iced water to retain the colour.

Put the red wine vinegar into a pan and bubble over a medium–high heat to reduce it until it becomes a thick glaze. Stir in the tomato purée, honey, sugar and olive oil, remove from the heat and leave to cool.

Once cool, stir through the aubergine, celery, mint, olives, oregano, sultanas, and mix well. Set aside.

In a small frying pan, gently fry the garlic in the tablespoon of olive oil until golden. Lift out the garlic (discard the oil) and leave to cool, then stir it into the caponata. Transfer the caponata to a bowl and leave in the fridge overnight.

The next day, lightly toast the pine nuts in a dry frying pan and crumble them over the top.

INSALATA DI RINFORZO

PICKLED VEGETABLE SALAD

THIS 'REINFORCEMENT' SALAD is one that you'll find on tables in Naples throughout the Christmas season. It's usually made as an *antipasti* for the Christmas Eve meal, when only fish and vegetables are served, then 'reinforced' with more vegetables and oil over the next week or so to keep it going until the New Year. *Borettane* onions are the saucer-like flat Italian onions, which have a mild, sweet flavour. You'll find the pickled variety is widely available in supermarkets, but use ordinary pickled onions if you can't get hold of them.

SERVES 8

400g romanesco cauliflower, *cut into bite-sized pieces*
400g white cauliflower, *cut into bite-sized pieces*
400g yellow cauliflower *(if available; otherwise just leave it out)*, *cut into bite-sized pieces*
400g purple sprouting broccoli, *cut into bite-sized pieces*
200g pickled borettane onions or standard pickled onions
50g sultanas
80g pickled caper berries
50ml extra virgin olive oil

FOR THE PICKLE BRINE
1 litre white wine vinegar
1 litre water
50g clear honey
45g sea salt
1 bay leaf
2 juniper berries
3 white peppercorns

Put all the pickle brine ingredients in a large pot and bring to the boil.

Cook each vegetable separately in the boiling brine for about 6–7 minutes, starting with the pale cauliflowers and cooking the purple sprouting broccoli last. Remove and drain each vegetable then let it cool and dry by laying it on a clean tea towel.

Put the cooled vegetables in a bowl, add the borettane onions, sultanas and capers and dress with the oil. This can be kept for up to a week in the fridge, making sure all the vegetables are covered in oil.

Opposite, from top left:
Cicoria catalogna,
rughetta, *bieta coste*
(Swiss chard), *cime di*
rapa, artichokes, Puglian
aubergines, sage.

VERDURE DI PUGLIA

PUGLIAN VEGETABLES

BEING CALABRESE, I probably shouldn't say this, but for me, one of the most beautiful and interesting regions in Italy, is Puglia – for the climate, for its history, for its spectacular unspoilt coastline, and of course, for its food. The versatility of the food in Puglia is remarkable: they have some of the best meat, the best fish and, most of all, what I think are the most beautiful vegetables in the world.

There is an area in northern Puglia called Il Tavoliere delle Puglie, which is the second biggest plain in Italy. It floods in the winter, meaning there is an abundance of water, yet due to the hot climate, it can be quite dry in the summer. Extensive work on the drainage system across the plain has made the ground extremely fertile and some of Puglia's most flavoursome vegetables are grown there. To discuss them all would require a book in itself so what follows is just the briefest of introductions to a few that I consider particularly characteristic of the region, and which I use a lot in my cooking.

Puntarelle, or *cicoria catalogna*, is a member of the chicory family – a head of feathery green curls with white and pale green stalks. It's a bitter green, similar to *cicoria tarassaco* (dandelion greens, see the recipe on page 180) and the two are interchangeable. The outer, slightly tough green leaves need to be cooked. They are usually blanched then sautéed before being mixed with other ingredients or plunged into a stew or soup. In Puglia and Calabria, you'll often see them piled on top of a popular dish called *macco di fave* (broad bean purée).

The pale green shoots that make up the core are usually sliced very thinly and eaten raw in a salad (such as the one on page 24). In this case, the preparation is important. Once you've stripped the outer leaves, you slice the shoots, then you need to leave them in iced water for at least an hour. The shoots will curl and become

THE VERSATILITY OF THE FOOD IN PUGLIA IS REMARKABLE: THEY HAVE SOME OF THE BEST MEAT AND FISH AND WHAT I THINK ARE THE MOST BEAUTIFUL VEGETABLES IN THE WORLD

beautifully crisp and that's how they should be enjoyed. You can also blanch and sauté the shoots and they make a very simple side dish dressed with salt and extra virgin olive oil.

Lampascioni are perhaps the most representative vegetable of Puglia. Though they look like button onions, they are in fact hyacinth bulbs, native to the region. They taste like a bitter onion too. They are usually found wild and harvested in the spring. The beautiful bulbs bury themselves quite deep in the earth so once they are dug up they need to be cleaned very thoroughly before use. My mum used to clean them one by one – running them under cold water and leaving them to soak for a couple of days, changing the water a few times, to remove all the dirt. Fresh, they can be fried in a similar way to onions, though remember they are bitter so they won't release sweetness in the same way. As a child, scrambled eggs with *lampascioni* and peppers was one of the 13 dishes we had as part of our Christmas Eve meal so they are particularly evocative for me; but they also pair particularly well with potatoes and with *baccalà*. However, the way you're most likely to encounter *lampascioni*, both in Puglia and in this country, is pickled. The Pugliese are masters of pickling – a Puglian *antipasti* would not be complete without a large selection of pickled vegetables – and *lampascioni* are a good candidate for being preserved in this way. You will struggle to find the fresh bulbs in this country but the pickled ones are available in Italian delis and you'll have no problem finding them online (see the list of stockists on page 286).

THE PUGLIESE ARE MASTERS OF PICKLING – A PUGLIAN *ANTIPASTI* WOULD NOT BE COMPLETE WITHOUT A LARGE SELECTION OF PICKLED VEGETABLES

Vivid green turnip tops – *cime di rapa* – are another leaf associated with Puglia, though they're widely used all over the South. One of Puglia's most characteristic dishes – *orechiette e cime di rapa* – partners the bitter green with the little ear-shaped pasta (see page 72), but it can be used in so many different ways - grilled, sautéed, stuffed into pizza...

VIVID GREEN *CIME DI RAPA* CAN BE USED IN SO MANY DIFFERENT WAYS – GRILLED, SAUTÉED, WITH PASTA OR STUFFED INTO PIZZA

Play with it. It's relatively easy to find *cime di rapa* in this country but you can use tenderstem broccoli, Brussels sprouts or other types of broccoli in its place if you can't. For more about *cime di rapa*, including when to seek it out, see page 178.

Opposite: Lampascioni

INSALATA DI MELANZANE

AUBERGINE SALAD

AUBERGINES HAVE BECOME inherently associated with the food of the South, and two of its most famous dishes – *caponata* and *pasta alla Norma* (see pages 190 and 71) take it as their leading light. It follows because Sicily is one of the first places in Europe that aubergines were grown after they were brought here by the Arabs. The round Italian aubergines I've suggested using can range in colour from deep purple to white and are still primarily grown in Sicily. The round variety have a meatier texture than the long purple ones we are more accustomed to seeing in this country, as well as fewer seeds and a slightly sweeter flavour so they're worth seeking out. They are available in the UK but you're most likely to find them at a farmers' market or specialist Italian deli.

The recipe here is like a lighter, pared back version of a *caponata* but suited to different uses. Serve it as part of a selection of salads alongside a pile of bruschetta; purée it to make a dip for vegetables and crusty bread; or use it as a stuffing for pasta shells. Make sure you cook the aubergines right through so they're very soft in the middle otherwise they'll blacken.

SERVES 4 — 6

2 round Italian aubergines (about 1kg), *halved*
1 long red chilli
1 tsp sea salt
juice of ½ lemon
10g salted capers, *soaked overnight*
50ml olive oil
5g mint, *roughly chopped*
5g marjoram, *roughly chopped*
5g flat-leaf parsley, *roughly chopped*

Preheat the oven to 200°C / fan 180°C / gas 6.

Bake the aubergines on a baking tray for 45 minutes to 1 hour or until soft right the way through.

Holding each aubergine half by the stalk, scoop the flesh out of the skin into a colander set over a bowl (discard the skin) then leave to drain until cooled to room temperature.

Heat a griddle pan over a high heat. Add the chilli and grill on all sides until lightly charred, then roughly chop into chunks.

Measure out 50ml of the aubergine juices and stir in the salt until dissolved. Add the lemon juice and capers then whisk in the olive oil to make a dressing.

Use your hands to break the aubergine flesh into large chunks and arrange on a serving dish. Drizzle the dressing over the top and garnish with the chopped herbs and the chilli.

CARCIOFI STUFATI

STEWED ARTICHOKES

I KNOW A LOT OF PEOPLE ARE PUT OFF BY ARTICHOKES because of the preparation but I can promise you that once you get a handle on this, it's not hard to do and the reward is well worth the effort. I absolutely love the thistly vegetable. This recipe is inspired by the Roman style of cooking artichokes – they are left whole and lightly braised in wine and stock, but it's got a hearty hit of the South too. I've stirred through cheese, breadcrumbs and anchovies at the end, which gives the dish richness and served with a green vegetable or salad makes the artichokes a meal in themselves. Let the artichokes cool to room temperature to serve – they'll continue to absorb all the braising liquid and expand. If you've never cooked artichokes before, make sure you taste them as you cook them – the amount of seasoning needed will vary and you want to make sure they're really tender before you turn off the heat.

SERVES 8

juice of 1 lemon
12 artichokes *(about 130–150g each), preferably mammole or violet (don't use globe)*
2 tbsp extra virgin olive oil
2 garlic cloves, *with skin, halved*
500ml white wine
1 litre vegetable stock
200g fresh peas
120g griotte onions
20g pecorino cheese, *grated*
10g mint, *roughly chopped*
10g flat-leaf parsley, *roughly chopped*
8 tinned anchovy fillets
20g fresh sourdough breadcrumbs, *left out at room temperature to go stale*
sea salt

Mix the lemon juice into a bowl of cold water. Clean each artichoke by picking off the external leaves until you reach the tender ones. Scoop out the hairy choke with a spoon (discard it) and peel the tough skin from the stalk. Place in the bowl of acidulated water to prevent discolouring.

Heat the oil in a saucepan over a medium heat and fry the garlic until golden, then lift out the garlic. Add the artichokes, increase the heat to high, season with salt and fry, stirring from time to time, until nice and golden.

Pour in the wine and stock, add the garlic, and let the liquid cook and evaporate slowly. After 6–7 minutes add the peas and the onions and continue to cook for about 4 minutes until the artichokes are soft and tender (taste a leaf to check).

Remove from the heat, then add the pecorino cheese, herbs, anchovies and breadcrumbs. Stir and allow the mixture to cool to room temperature – the artichokes will reabsorb the liquid.

FIORI DI ZUCCA RIPIENI

COURGETTE FLOWERS STUFFED WITH RICOTTA

COURGETTE FLOWERS are one of the most sexy and beautiful foods in the world. This is the classic recipe for stuffing them – a simple lemony ricotta that's warmed by the heat of the frying. If you're not a fan of deep-frying, you can just stuff the flowers and bake them in the oven but I recommend you try it at least once – the light, crisp batter is a fantastic contrast to the delicate flowers and smooth filling. To bake, lay the stuffed flowers on a baking tray, brush with melted butter and scatter with pecorino then cook at 210°C / fan 190°C / gas 7 (with the overhead grill on too if you can) for about 8 minutes or until golden. You want the stem to be crunchy but nice and hot in the middle.

SERVES 4

12 courgette flowers *(as large as you can find),*
  still attached to the baby courgettes
250g fresh ricotta cheese
25g pecorino cheese
grated zest of ½ unwaxed lemon
about 1.5 litres sunflower oil
sea salt and freshly ground black pepper
Chilli Jam *(see page 274), to serve*

FOR THE BATTER

300g '00' flour
pinch of sea salt
1 egg yolk
7g fresh yeast
480ml lager *(I would use Ichnusa or Menabrea*
  beer but use the lager of your choice)

For the batter, put the flour and salt into a large bowl. In another bowl mix the egg yolk, yeast and half the lager, and use a hand whisk to stir this into the flour. Add the rest of the lager and whisk well. Cover with cling film and leave on the side to double in size – it will take about a couple of hours.

In the meantime, remove the stamen from the flowers and gently open out the trumpets.

Put the ricotta, pecorino cheese and the lemon zest into a bowl and season well with salt and pepper.

Use a teaspoon to carefully fill the flowers with the cheese mixture, making sure to leave some space at the top to seal the flower, then twist the tops to close.

Heat the sunflower oil in a deep saucepan or fat fryer large enough to fit the length of the flower, to 190°C. Dip each flower in the batter, letting the excess drop off and deep-fry the flowers on each side until golden brown. Carefully remove and drain on kitchen paper. Serve hot with the chilli jam.

PIPI E PATATE

POTATOES WITH DRIED CHILLIES

THIS DISH IS SUCH AN INHERENT PART of the *mezzogiorno* region's cuisine that there are songs written about it. All South Italians will have grown up eating this, although how many of us ate it as it was traditionally made – in a *frissura* pan over the fire – is perhaps declining. My grandmother used to wake up at 5am to feed the pigs and other animals, so by 10am she was hungry; this was her second breakfast. The slow-cooked spicy potatoes and peppers are rich and sustaining and with a fried egg in the middle, as I like to serve them, this is indulgent comfort food. Without the egg the potatoes are a great accompaniment to barbecued pork ribs or grilled lamb chops.

SERVES 4

1kg Cyprus, King Edward or Maris Piper potatoes, *peeled*
10g dried chilli
700g Romano peppers, *halved, deseeded and cut into strips*
100g white onion, *finely sliced*
150ml extra virgin olive oil
2 tsp fine salt
1 tsp dried oregano

Cut the potatoes into 2mm slices and place in a big bowl. Crush the dried chilli and add it to the potatoes, then add the pepper, onion, oil and salt and mix well.

Heat a large non-stick pan over a medium heat and add the potato mixture. Cook, stirring frequently, until the potatoes are cooked through and are golden brown and crisp.

Transfer to a serving dish, scatter over the oregano and serve.

VERDURE GRIGLIATE ALL`ORIGANO

GRILLED VEGETABLES WITH OREGANO

THIS DISH SIMPLY HAS TO BE COOKED USING A BARBECUE.
A barbecue allows you to cook the vegetables directly over the heat without any oil. There are so many advantages to this – firstly you won't burn a beautiful olive oil with heat, and the vegetables won't soak it up and become soggy. Cooked this way you add the oil to the vegetables at the end, as a dressing, which means you can control the flavours. I like my vegetables cut into chunks so that they don't lose all their water, and cooked until they're very black and charred, which is how you can pack in flavour.

SERVES 4—6 AS A MAIN COURSE, ABOUT 8 AS A SIDE

300g fennel bulb, *trimmed*
160g trimmed leeks
500g peppers, *halved and cut into 4—6 wedges*
300g aubergines, *sliced into rounds 1.5cm thick*
200g tomatoes, *sliced*
300g courgettes, *sliced lengthways 1.5cm thick*
1 red chilli, *cut in half*
1 green chilli, *cut in half*
sea salt

FOR THE DRESSING
150ml extra virgin olive oil
75ml red wine vinegar
2 tsp clear honey
10g mint
10g fresh oregano
2 garlic cloves
½ tsp dried oregano
½ tsp sea salt

Preheat the oven to 210°C/fan 190°C/gas 7. Prepare your barbecue.

Cut the fennel into wedges and the leeks into slices of about 1.5cm, grill on the barbecue until blackened, then transfer to a baking sheet and finish cooking in the oven for about 10 minutes – this will ensure the centres are cooked through.

In a bowl, whisk together all the ingredients for the dressing and leave aside.

Season all the remaining vegetables with salt and barbecue them until charred and tender, then transfer to a large serving dish with the fennel and the leeks and pour over the dressing. Leave for 10 minutes for the flavours to penetrate and settle, then serve.

6
DOLCI

ZEPPOLE
AL PISTACCHIO

PASTRY RINGS FILLED WITH PISTACHIO CREAM

ITALY'S CATHOLIC CALENDAR means there are plenty of cakes and pastries linked to particular feast days or celebrations. *Zeppole* are associated with Saint Joseph's Day, March 19th, which is also Father's Day, and they are often sold in the street or given as gifts. The Neapolitan pastries – rings of dough, filled with a flavoured pastry cream, custard or ricotta – can be baked or deep-fried. Plain custard ones are traditionally finished with a dollop of custard on the outside topped with a glacé cherry, while this pistachio version would have a single nut sitting on its crown of green cream.

You will most likely need to buy the pistachio paste for the filling online, but it's not difficult to make your own. Simply toast 150g shelled pistachio nuts in an oven preheated to 180°C/fan 160°C/gas 4, then, while they are hot, whizz them in a small blender or processor until the nuts are finely ground. Continue to whizz until the mixture becomes an oily paste. There's more than enough for this recipe, but the paste works well stirred into yoghurt or spread on toast.

SERVES 8

FOR THE PISTACHIO CREAM
1 gelatine leaf
60g caster sugar
3 egg yolks
10g strong bread flour
10g cornflour
200ml full-fat milk
50g pistachio paste (*shop-bought or see the introduction for how to make your own*)
½ vanilla pod, *split in half, seeds scraped*
grated zest of 1 lemon
200ml double cream
shelled pistachio nuts, *to decorate (optional)*

Start by making the pistachio cream. Soak the gelatine leaf in water, making sure it's completely immersed.

In a large bowl, whisk the sugar and egg yolks until pale and creamy, then whisk in the flour and cornflour.

Bring the milk to the boil in a large saucepan. When boiling, turn off the heat and add half the milk to the egg mixture, whisking constantly. When fully combined, return this mixture to the pan with the rest of the milk; this prevents the eggs scrambling. Place back on a medium heat and whisk rapidly and continuously, until boiling. Take off the heat immediately and continue whisking for another minute so that it doesn't stick to the bottom of the pan.

Drain the gelatine and squeeze out any excess water, then add it to the custard mixture along with the pistachio paste, vanilla seeds and lemon zest. Mix well to combine, then transfer to a bowl, cover the surface with cling film to prevent a skin forming and chill until cold. The longer you can leave it, the more it will firm up, making it easier to pipe.

FOR THE CHOUX PASTRY

150g full-fat milk
150g water
130g unsalted butter, *chopped*
170g strong bread flour, *sifted three times*
15g caster sugar
5g salt
3–4 medium eggs

Now make the pastry. Preheat the oven to 190°C/fan 170°C/gas 5. Line two baking trays with baking paper. Draw 8 circles on the paper using an 8cm round cutter then turn over so the markings are on the other side. Make sure there's enough space between each one so that the pastry rings won't stick together as they expand when they cook.

Put the milk, water and butter into a saucepan. Heat gently to melt the butter then increase the heat and bring to a rolling boil. Add the flour, sugar and salt and stir the mixture quickly and continuously with a wooden spoon until the mixture forms a ball of dough that comes away from the sides of the pan.

Transfer the dough to a bowl and set aside to cool until the underside of the bowl is no longer too hot to touch and the mixture feels just warm.

Add the eggs one by one, whisking rapidly after each addition. Make sure each egg is fully incorporated before adding the next otherwise the mixture will split. As you add the egg, the mixture will become glossy but should still be stiff. If it's becoming too loose, stop adding eggs; if it's too stiff add a little more egg. To check this, lift a spoonful of the pastry with a spatula; it should form a teardrop shape but shouldn't be dropping off. Transfer to a piping bag fitted with a 2cm nozzle (or cut a 2cm width across the end of a plastic piping bag).

Using the marked rings as a guide, pipe the mixture around each line, then pipe another circle on top. Repeat until you've made 8 rings. Bake for 30–35 minutes, until crisp, golden and a ring sounds hollow when tapped. Push a knife into the side of each ring along the natural crease and return the trays to the oven for 5 minutes to allow the inside of the choux rings to dry out. Then remove from the oven, transfer to a wire rack to cool completely.

When everything is ready to assemble, use a balloon whisk to blend the cold custard until smooth. In another bowl, whip the double cream until it's thick and forms stiff peaks. Fold the custard into the double cream and mix until fully combined. Transfer to a piping bag fitted with a 2cm nozzle (or snip the end as before).

To assemble, slice the choux rings in half horizontally then pipe the cream into one half of each ring. Cover with their lids, then pipe a walnut-sized piece of cream on the outside, and top with a pistachio, if you like.

CANNOLI SICILIANI

THE CLASSIC SICILIAN DESSERT; no trip to the island is complete without trying one of the rolls of deep-fried pastry filled with sweetened ricotta. One of my most memorable food experiences was during a trip to the Vucciria market in Palermo. I watched a vendor making up the fattest *cannoli* I have ever seen. Mesmerised, I stared as he deep-fried the pastry while mixing the ricotta with orange zest, icing sugar, candied fruit, cinnamon and grated chocolate before stuffing the hot roll and dipping the ends in chopped pistachio. It was one of the most amazing things I've ever tasted.

Nowadays you can buy pre-made *cannoli* shells, so it's even easier to make them at home, but as with everything, fresh is so much better. Resting the pastry overnight is extremely important; it's what allows the *cannoli's* characteristic bubbles to form.

You will need at least two metal *cannoli* rings – 14cm long and 2cm in diameter.

MAKES 10

FOR THE PASTRY
170g strong flour
40g unsalted butter, *softened*
2 tbsp beaten egg, *plus a little extra for securing the dough*
2 medium egg yolks
15g caster sugar
1g salt
2 tsp Marsala
1½–2 litres sunflower oil, *for deep-frying*

FOR THE FILLING
350g fresh sheep's ricotta (or cow's if unavailable), *drained and passed through a sieve*
100g icing sugar, *plus extra to dust*
¼ tsp ground cinnamon
grated zest of ½ orange
15g each of chopped pistachios, chopped dark chocolate and chopped candied peel

Sift the flour into a bowl. Make a well in the centre and add the butter, beaten egg, egg yolks, sugar and salt. Mix everything together with a table knife until it looks like a crumble. You can also do this stage in a stand mixer using the K blade, if you like.

Add the Marsala and mix well again until the mixture forms a dough. Bring the mixture together with your hands and knead very gently then shape into a flat disc, wrap in cling film and refrigerate overnight.

The next day, take the dough out of the fridge and set aside at room temperature for about an hour for the dough to warm up and soften slightly.

Pour the oil into a deep-fat fryer or deep saucepan and heat until it reaches 180°C. Divide the dough into 10 even portions and roll one piece out on a lightly floured board until it's about 2mm thick. It's best to do it this way so that you ensure you get even rounds. Use a 10cm scone cutter to cut out one round. Wrap it around the metal cannoli ring, securing the end with a little beaten egg. Repeat until you've covered as many cannoli rings as you have – you may have to set aside some of the pastry circles and wait to wrap them if all the metal rings are being used. If you have time, leave the dough to rest on the rings for 20 minutes – this helps the dough to relax again so you'll get those characteristic bubbles on the pastry.

continued overleaf

Using the basket of your fryer or a slotted spoon, gently lower a ring into the oil, until the whole thing is submerged. Fry for 3–4 minutes until golden, then remove and transfer to a plate lined with kitchen towel, to drain and cool. When each ring is cool enough for you to hold it, carefully slip the cannoli off its ring. Repeat until you have cooked all 10 rolls. Leave to cool completely before filling.

Mix the ricotta, icing sugar, cinnamon and orange zest together in a bowl then spoon into a disposable piping bag. Cut about 1cm off the end and pipe the filling into the pastry rings.

Put the chocolate, pistachio and candied peel into saucers and dip each cannoli end in a different one – traditionally they don't match. Dust with icing sugar and serve immediately.

TORTA CIOCCOLATO E PEPERONCINO

CHOCOLATE AND CHILLI CAKE

SICILY'S TURBULENT HISTORY is closely intertwined with the Spanish, and in the town of Modica, the influence of the period of Spanish rule is reflected in the town's oldest chocolate factory. At the Antica Dolceria Bonajuto, they still make chocolate according to the ancient Aztec methods introduced to the island by the Spanish in the fifteenth century. Cacao beans were ground up to produce a 'cacao flour' that was then mixed with spices, such as cinnamon, vanilla and chilli before being set. Today at the factory they still sell bars made in a similar way, with these flavours, and it was their chilli chocolate that inspired this cake. The gentle heat from the chilli heightens and warms the flavour of the chocolate and the result is a cake that's dense and very chocolatey but not too strong. Serve it with some mascarpone mixed with icing sugar and chopped basil leaves or lemon zest if you want a cooling contrast.

SERVES 12

100g unsalted butter, *plus extra for greasing the tin*
110g dark chocolate *(minimum 70 per cent cocoa solids)*
2 bird's eye chillies, *deseeded and finely chopped*
3 medium eggs
120g caster sugar
135g ground almonds

Preheat the oven to 160°C/fan 140°C/gas 3. Grease an 18cm cake tin with butter and line the bottom with baking paper.

Place the butter, chocolate and chilli in a heatproof bowl set over a pan of just simmering water, making sure the bottom of the bowl doesn't touch the water. Heat gently to allow the chocolate and butter to melt then stir the ingredients together carefully to combine. Set aside to cool a little.

Whisk the eggs and sugar together in a large bowl with an electric whisk until very pale and fluffy. This will take about 10–15 minutes. Gently fold the butter and chocolate mixture into the eggs with a spatula, followed by the ground almonds.

Pour into the cake tin and bake for 40–50 minutes. To check it's ready, insert a skewer in the centre – it should come out almost clean. It won't come out completely clean as it is a moist cake.

Leave to cool in the tin for about 10 minutes, then turn out on to a wire rack and allow to cool completely.

MELANZANE E CIOCCOLATO

AUBERGINE AND CHOCOLATE CAKE

YOU'RE PROBABLY THINKING this sounds like a very strange combination, but southern Italians like to mix sweet and savoury – it's our Moorish legacy, and I'm pretty sure you'll be surprised by how well the aubergine works in a cake. Its mild, smoky flavour is simply complemented by the chocolate and above all it just gives the cake a beautifully moist, fudgy consistency. The idea for this cake comes from a traditional Neapolitan recipe, which you'll see served along the Amalfi Coast, particularly around the 15th August, Italy's national day. Layers of fried aubergine are dipped in sugar, spread with chocolate and sometimes ricotta. It is very unusual but is a real treasure from South Italy and I'd like to see the concept live on.

SERVES 12

1kg aubergines, *cut in half lengthways*
4 mint leaves, *finely chopped*
240g caster sugar
200g unsalted butter
225g dark chocolate *(minimum 70 per cent cocoa solids)*
6 eggs
140g ground hazelnuts *(if you can't buy them see page 241 for how to make your own)*

Preheat the oven to 200°C / fan 180°C / gas 6. Place the aubergine halves on a baking tray and cook until the flesh is really soft and the skin is burnt – it should take 30–45 minutes.

Transfer the aubergine to a bowl, cover with cling film, leave to cool then scoop the flesh out of the skin and discard the skin. Place in a sieve for a few hours to drain the liquid so that most of it is gone. Finally, roughly chop the aubergine and stir through the mint.

Heat the oven to 160°C / fan 140°C / gas 3. Grease a 23cm cake tin with butter and line the bottom with baking paper.

Place the butter and chocolate in a heatproof bowl set over a pan of just simmering water, making sure the bottom of the bowl doesn't touch the water. Heat gently to allow the chocolate and butter to melt then stir together carefully to combine. Set aside to cool a little.

Whisk the eggs and sugar together in a large bowl with an electric whisk until very pale and fluffy. This will take about 10–15 minutes. Gently fold the butter and chocolate mixture into the eggs with a spatula, followed by the ground hazelnuts.

Put the aubergine into a separate bowl, add about an eighth of the chocolate mixture and mix very well, then fold this into the rest of the chocolate mixture. Pour into the cake tin and bake for 1–1½ hours. To check it's ready, insert a skewer in the centre – it should come out almost clean. It won't come out completely clean as it is a moist cake. Leave to cool in the tin for about 10 minutes, then turn out on to a wire rack and allow to cool completely.

DELIZIA DI LIMONE

LEMON CAKE

THE AMALFI COASTLINE boasts some of the most beautiful lemons in the world – plump, juicy, fragrant and flavoursome, so this traditional Neapolitan dessert is a decadent celebration of its region's treasures. Small light sponge cakes are soaked in limoncello syrup then layered and topped with a bright yellow lemon custard. It's a striking addition to a table, particularly if you decorate the top with lemon leaves, and is a popular dessert at weddings as each guest receives their own ready-portioned round of cake.

SERVES 12

FOR THE BOTTOM AND MIDDLE SPONGE LAYER
butter, *for greasing*
4 medium eggs
140g caster sugar
150g plain flour
4g baking powder

FOR THE TOP SPONGE LAYER
1 medium egg
35g caster sugar
40g plain flour
1g baking powder

FOR THE LEMON CUSTARD
750ml milk
grated zest of 1 lemon
6 medium egg yolks
6 tbsp caster sugar
6 tbsp plain flour
175ml double cream, *lightly whipped to soft peaks*

Preheat the oven to 180°C / fan 160°C / gas mark 4.

For the bottom and middle layers of sponge, grease two 30 × 21cm shallow rectangular tins (or use Swiss roll tins) and line the bases with greaseproof paper.

Beat the eggs and sugar together in a mixer until the mixture looks pale and fluffy. Sift the flour and baking powder over the top and carefully fold into the mixture using a large metal spoon.

Divide the mixture evenly between the tins and level the surface – it should be very thin. Bake for 15 minutes until golden and the sponge is soft. Turn each sponge out of its tin on to a wire rack to cool.

Next, make the top layer of sponge. Grease and line the base of a 20cm round cake tin with greaseproof paper. Beat the egg and sugar together in a stand mixer until the mixture looks pale and moussey. Sift the flour and baking powder over the top and carefully fold into the mixture using a large metal spoon. Spoon into the tin and level the surface. Bake for 15 minutes, until golden, then turn out of the tin on to a wire rack to cool.

Now make the custard. Bring the milk and lemon to the boil in a small saucepan. Whisk the egg yolks and sugar until combined, then add the flour. When the milk is piping hot, slowly stir it into the egg until combined. Return it to the pan and cook over a medium heat until it becomes a thick custard. Spoon into a bowl, cover the custard completely with cling film to stop a skin from forming. Allow to cool then chill.

continued overleaf

FOR THE SPONGE SYRUP
50ml water
50g caster sugar
25ml limoncello liqueur

TO DECORATE
lemon leaves
strands of lemon zest

For the syrup, put the water and sugar together in a small pan and heat gently to dissolve the sugar. Bring to the boil and simmer for 2–3 minutes until syrupy. Take the pan off the heat and leave to cool. Once cool, stir in the limoncello.

Use a 7cm scone cutter to cut 12 rounds out of each rectangle of sponge. Then use a 3.5cm round to cut 12 small circles out of the round sponge (the base of a piping nozzle is ideal). Brush 12 of the large rounds with the syrup then arrange on a large platter in a rectangle.

Fold the whipped cream into the custard using a large metal spoon and carefully whisk using a balloon whisk until smooth. Use a teaspoon to spread a spoonful of the lemon custard over each round. Brush the remaining 12 large rounds with syrup and place on top; cover with custard as before.

Brush the little rounds with syrup and arrange one on top of each round of covered sponge. Now spoon the remaining custard over each round to cover, making sure there are no gaps.

Use any leftover custard to pipe a small blob in between each space of sponge to fill in the holes, then decorate the cake with lemon leaves and curls of lemon zest.

CREMA DI RICOTTA E FICO DOTTATO COSENTINO

RICOTTA WITH MARINATED DOTTATO FIGS

THIS IS A SIMPLE DESSERT but ideally it should be made with very fresh sheep's ricotta. The flavour of sheep's ricotta is not to everybody's taste – it's much stronger and richer than cow's, but here the flavour is tempered by the mascarpone, cream and sugar, so it's a good way to try it in a milder context. Do just use double the amount of cow's ricotta if you can't get hold of sheep's.

The type of fig used is important. I've specified *dottato* figs, which are a particularly sweet variety of Calabrian fig from Cosenza; you will find them in larger Italian delis and online (see the stockists list on page 286). They are picked in July and August then left to dry in the sun, or now more commonly, very slowly baked in the oven, which makes them dark, sticky and sweet with a very intense fig flavour.

Here they're plumped by gently heating them in *saba* (fig nectar) syrup but you could use Marsala or *mosto cotto* in its place. The ricotta cream and the crunchy pistachio brittle add wonderful textural contrasts.

SERVES 6 — 8

FOR THE PISTACHIO CROCCANTE
100g whole shelled pistachios
200g caster sugar
50g liquid glucose

FOR THE FIGS
210g dottato figs *(or other dried figs, if unavailable)*
50g blossom honey
50ml dark rum
100ml water
120g saba (fig nectar)
grated zest of ½ orange

Start by making the pistachio croccante. Heat the oven to 220°C / fan 200°C / gas 7. Line a baking tray with baking paper.

Toast the pistachios on a baking sheet for 10 minutes. Transfer to a bowl and leave to cool, then roughly chop.

Place the sugar in a saucepan and heat until a thermometer reads 170°C, or until it has become a golden to bronze caramel. Add the glucose then the pistachios and mix rapidly. Pour on to the piece of baking paper and cover with another piece. Use a rolling pin to roll the croccante as thin as possible, then leave to cool.

Put all the fig ingredients in a saucepan. Bring to a simmer on a medium heat, with a lid on, and simmer for about 30 minutes or until the figs are soft all the way through.

Remove the figs and their syrup from the pan and leave to cool.

continued overleaf

FOR THE RICOTTA CREAM
150g cow's ricotta
150g sheep's ricotta *(or use double the amount of cow's ricotta if you can't find sheep's)*
30g icing sugar
100g double cream
100g mascarpone
grated zest of ½ orange
pinch of ground cinnamon

Mix the ricotta and icing sugar until combined. Whip the double cream to stiff peaks, then gently fold in all the remaining ingredients with a spatula until you have a thick mousse-like consistency.

To serve, cut the figs in half and arrange on serving plates. Spoon some of the cream on the side. Drizzle with syrup and serve with a piece of croccante, or just leave it in the middle and get everybody to break off their own.

TORRONE AL PISTACCHIO

PISTACHIO NOUGAT

TORRONE IS TRADITIONALLY SERVED AT CHRISTMAS TIME and there are regional variations across Italy – squidgy, firm, covered in chocolate, most commonly filled with almonds, but often with other nuts. This is the version I grew up with – a soft and sticky pistachio nougat coated in dark chocolate. Addictive.

MAKES ABOUT 40 PIECES, DEPENDING ON HOW BIG YOU CUT THEM

butter, *for greasing*
180g caster sugar
55g liquid glucose
40ml water
130g blossom honey or another good-flavoured runny honey
2 large egg whites
1 vanilla pod, *split in half lengthways, seeds scraped*
190g unsalted pistachios
150g dark chocolate *(minimum 70 per cent cocoa solids)*

Grease and line a 21cm square tin with baking paper.

Put the sugar, glucose and water into a small heavy-based saucepan and heat gently to dissolve the sugar. Bring the mixture to the boil, then continue to boil until the mixture reaches 157°C. At the same time, bring the honey to the boil in a separate pan.

Meanwhile, using a stand mixer, whisk the egg whites until they form soft peaks, then while continuing to whisk, slowly add the sugar mixture, pouring it down the sides of the bowl, so that the beaters don't send hot sugar flying, then add the honey in the same way.

Add the vanilla seeds and continue to whisk on a medium speed for about 10 minutes until the mixture forms soft peaks and the outside of the bowl has cooled to just warm. Fold in the pistachios with a large metal spoon.

Spoon into the tin and level the surface with the back of the spoon. Set aside to cool completely for 2 hours.

Once the torrone has set, place the chocolate in a heatproof bowl set over a pan of simmering water (don't let the bottom of the bowl touch the water) and allow it to melt.

Pour over the top of the torrone, making sure it covers the whole surface, and leave for about 4 hours, until set. Remove the torrone from the tin and put on a board. Use a long sharp chopping knife to cut into bite-size pieces, around 2.5 × 3cm.

BRIOSCIA E GELATO

BRIOCHE AND ICE CREAM

WHILE IN THE REST OF THE COUNTRY, we might look on a brioche bun stuffed with ice cream as a dessert or afternoon snack, for the Sicilians it's breakfast. Wander around any town or village on a summer's morning and you're likely to see locals tucking into this rich yet refreshing delicacy alongside their cappuccino. You'll find that the bun is sturdier than a buttery, soft French brioche as it needs to be able to soak up some of the ice cream without going soggy. For Sicilians, the morning stuffing is likely to be some kind of *granita*, usually almond, but as the day goes on, choices turn to creamier *gelati*.

And a note about scooping: in Italy, we don't really use ice cream scoops – palette knives or spoons are what you'll see being used in the *gelaterie* because ice cream isn't about being neat or precise and you can pack a lot more into the bread, on to the cone, or into the *coppa*, which is the most important thing.

MAKES ABOUT 15 BUNS

FOR THE BRIOCHE
10g fresh yeast or 5g dried active yeast
50g caster sugar
125g whole milk
500g '00' flour
10g salt
125g water
7g malt
3 medium egg yolks, plus an extra beaten egg yolk,
    to glaze
50g unsalted butter, *at room temperature,*
    cut into dice
2 vanilla pods, *halved lengthways, seeds scraped*

TO SERVE
Any of the ice creams or sorbets on pages 240–246

Put the yeast and ½ teaspoon of the sugar into a small bowl. Gently heat the milk until lukewarm and pour about 3 tablespoons over the yeast. Set aside for 10 minutes, until the yeast has activated and is frothy.

Sift the flour into the bowl of a stand mixer fitted with the dough hook. Add the salt.

In a jug, whisk together the water, remaining milk and sugar in a jug, along with the malt and egg yolks. Pour into the bowl of the mixer, then pour in the activated yeast mixture.

Mix with a dough hook on the lowest speed for 6 minutes, then increase the speed to medium and continue to mix for 15 minutes. The dough will be nice and smooth.

Add the butter and vanilla seeds and continue to mix until the butter has all been incorporated. Cover the bowl and leave for 30 minutes to allow the dough to rise.

Line two baking sheets with baking parchment. Lift the dough on to a board and divide into 4 even pieces. Divide the dough into pieces weighing 50g each, then divide the remainder into small pieces of 7g each. Roll all the pieces into balls and place on the parchment. Do the same again with the other three large pieces of dough.

continued overleaf

Cover the trays and leave to prove in a warm place for about 2 hours, or until doubled in size.

Heat the oven to 200°C/fan 180°C/gas 6. Use a little water to stick a small ball on top of each larger ball. Brush the buns with the egg yolk glaze then bake for 30–45 minutes, turning the trays halfway through baking, until the buns are golden and sound hollow when tapped on the bottom. Remove from the oven and leave to cool completely.

To serve, slice the brioche almost completely in half horizontally (leave the back edge attached). Spread a spoonful of ice cream or sorbet into the middle and serve immediately.

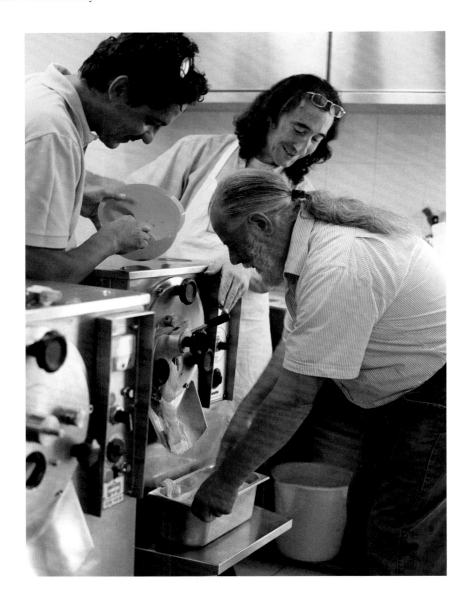

CASSATA

BAKED RICOTTA TART

SICILY IS RENOWNED THROUGHOUT ITALY for the skills of its pastry makers and its islanders' sweet teeth, and *cassata*, along with *cannoli* (see page 212) are two of its most iconic pastries. The recipe here is the original, older version, which is made with the obligatory sheep's ricotta and candied fruit, but they are baked in a pastry case. The version you are more likely to find in Sicily these days covers the fresh, uncooked cheese with marzipan and decorates the top with candied fruit. Making that version is quite a chore, and is something most Sicilians would buy from a *pasticceria*, while this one is very simple to make. It's best enjoyed with a glass of cold Marsala wine.

SERVES 12

FOR THE FILLING
250g ricotta
40g icing sugar, *plus extra for dusting*
1 medium egg yolk
⅛ tsp ground cinnamon
¼–½ tsp orange blossom water
40g candied citrus peel, *chopped*
40g dark chocolate (*70 per cent cocoa solids*), *chopped*

FOR THE SWEET PASTRY
100g unsalted butter, *softened*
70g icing sugar
1 medium egg yolk
170g plain flour

For the filling, rest a sieve over a large bowl and spoon in the ricotta. Transfer to the refrigerator and leave to drain while you make the pastry.

Put the butter, icing sugar and egg yolk in a food processor. Add half the flour and whizz to make a very rough dough. Add the remaining flour and whizz again until the mixture forms a dough and comes together. Tip on to a board and bring together with your hands. Shape into a large flat disc and wrap in greaseproof paper (this helps with rolling out later) and chill for about 1½ hours, ideally overnight, until firm.

Preheat the oven to 200°C / 180°c fan / gas mark 6. Have ready a 21cm × 2.5cm fluted tart tin.

Unwrap the dough, slice off about a third and set aside, wrapped in cling film, then roll the rest of it out until it is around 3mm thick. Carefully lift the edge of the pastry up over a rolling pin and lift into the tin. Press it down to line the base and sides of the tin, then trim the excess so that you have a neat finish around the top. Prick the base with a fork. Chill for 1 hour.

Line the pastry case with greaseproof paper and fill it with baking beans. Bake for 10 minutes, or until a pale golden, then remove the beans and return the tin to the oven to bake for 5 minutes more until the base feels dry to the touch. Remove from the oven, and leave to cool completely.

Put the drained ricotta, icing sugar, egg yolk, cinnamon and orange water into a bowl and whisk until combined. Fold in the citrus peel and dark chocolate. Spoon into the pastry case and level the top. Roll out the reserved pastry until 3mm thick then use the base of a 21cm cake tin as a template to cut a round out of the pastry. Using the rolling pin to balance the pastry on it, carefully lift the round on top of the tin to cover the ricotta filling. Push a table knife into the middle and make two small slashes for the steam to escape.

Bake for another 30 minutes, until golden. Leave to cool in the tin until just warm, then flip out upside-down on to a board or large serving platter, dust with plenty of icing sugar and serve nice big slices.

M'PIGLIATI

CALABRIAN 'MINCE PIES'

IN ACCORDANCE WITH THE CUCINA POVERA TRADITION,
pastry in the South is very often made using pork fat (lard), which is not only
a way of avoiding waste, but also of adding a bit of richness and flavour (if you
don't like the idea you can easily use butter or olive oil instead).

These small pastries are quite dry on their own – the paste in the middle
is similar to a sticky mince pie filling and they have quite a generous amount of
pastry – but to serve them, you drench them with *mosto cotto*, which makes them
beautifully moist. It also means that the pastries will keep for a couple of weeks
if you store them in an airtight container – just keep feeding them with *mosto
cotto* like you would a Christmas cake.

This might sound strange but I usually have my *m'pigliata* with a slice of
pecorino as I like the sweet and savoury combination. However, they're usually
served with a glass of Marsala, and are often the *dolci* we serve to friends who
drop by in the afternoon.

MAKES 7

FOR THE PASTRY
2 eggs
500g strong flour
1 tsp baking powder
1 tbsp grappa
1 tbsp Marsala
200g whipping cream
10g lard or olive oil or butter, *at room temperature*

FOR THE FILLING
50g walnuts
50g hazelnuts
50g pistachios
50g dried figs, *roughly chopped*
50g dried apricots, *roughly chopped*
150g blossom honey

TO FINISH
2 egg yolks, beaten
250ml mosto cotto *(grape must syrup)*

Mix all the pastry ingredients together using a spatula until fully
combined. You should have a soft but not sticky dough. Form the
dough into a ball, cover with cling film and chill overnight.

For the filling, put the nuts and dried fruit into a food processor and
pulse until finely chopped. Add the honey and pulse again until you
have a chunky paste. Chill overnight.

The next day, heat the oven to 220°C / fan 200°C / gas 7. Line a baking
tray with baking paper.

On a lightly floured work surface or using a pasta machine, roll the
pastry into a rectangle 1mm thick. The pasta machine is the easiest
way to ensure it's thin enough; you should almost see your hand
through it when you lift it up. Trim the edges and cut the pastry into
strips of 25 × 4cm (I used a crimped pastry cutter for the picture)
then brush them with the beaten egg yolk.

Dust a work surface very lightly with icing sugar, then roll the filling
into 1.5cm-diameter sausages long enough to fit the length of the
pastry (25cm). Lay the rolls down the middle of each pastry strip,
wrap the pastry up around it and brush the top and sides with more
beaten egg so that they stick together. Carefully roll the filled pastry
into a pinwheel shape. Repeat – you should have seven pinwheels.
Place on the lined tray and bake for 25 – 30 minutes, until golden
brown. Transfer to a wire rack to cool. Once cool, drizzle over the
mosto cotto (they should be drenched) and serve.

CARTELLATTE

PUGLIAN FRIED PASTRY

A LOVE OF FRITTELLE (FRIED PASTRY) is something that is shared by northern and southern Italians, except that every cook and region has their own idea of what they should be. Puglia's striking rose-shaped spirals are typically festive, usually eaten throughout December, in celebration of their town's saint – Nicholas.

The pastry needs to be rolled out paper-thin ('*carta*' means paper) to keep it as crisp as possible. Don't be worried about shaping them neatly – they're meant to look fairly rustic. And serve them with a LOT of *mosto cotto*; they are meant to be drenched. If you can't find *mosto cotto*, *cartellatte* are served with honey or *saba* (fig nectar) too.

SERVES 6 — 8

500g '00' flour
2 eggs
1 tsp baking powder
1 tbsp Marsala wine
1 tbsp grappa
12g lard, *at room temperature*
300ml mosto cotto (grape must syrup)
1 tsp ground cinnamon
about 1.5 litres sunflower oil, *for deep-frying*

Mix all the ingredients except the mosto cotto and cinnamon, until you have a smooth dough. Shape it into a ball, wrap in cling film and leave in the fridge overnight.

Using a rolling pin or a pasta machine, roll out the dough until it's about 2–3mm thick. Using a crimped pastry cutter cut the dough into strips of 30 x 3cm. Pinch the long sides of the strips together every 3cm to form little pockets. Keeping these pockets upright, roll the pastry from one of the short ends to form a spiral shape, pinching the pockets together to make them stick (wet your fingers if necessary).

While you finish shaping all the cartellate, heat a large deep pan with the sunflower oil until it reaches 170°C.

Fry the cartellate in batches – don't overcrowd the pan otherwise the temperature of the oil will drop and they will end up soggy not crisp. When they are a golden brown colour, remove and place in a tray lined with kitchen paper to absorb the excess oil. Continue to fry all the cartellate.

When they are all completely cool, transfer them to a serving dish, drizzle over the mosto cotto, dust them with the cinnamon and serve.

LIQUIRIZIA

LIQUORICE

I IMAGINE the word immediately makes you think of the sticky, black interiors of the Bassett's Allsorts, or the salty Scandinavian sweets, but Italy has a long and passionate association with growing liquorice thanks to Calabria. It is an important export for the region and one of the elements that most distinguishes our cooking from the rest of the *mezzogiorno* area.

The Calabrian microclimate is particularly suited to growing liquorice, and this, combined with its distinctive soil composition, into which the roots dig deep, provide the perfect conditions for an intensely flavoured liquorice that is thought to be among the best in the world. Liquorice literally means 'sweet root' and indeed it is the strong roots of the delicate plant that are harvested, however the plant needs to have been established for at least four years and its roots must measure 1–2 metres before you can cut them.

THE AMARELLI FAMILY HAVE BEEN HARVESTING LIQUORICE SINCE THE SIXTEENTH CENTURY

The fresh roots have a very intense aromatic flavour and can only be used to infuse marinades or drinks (then removed) or chewed to extract the juices. The dried roots, which is how you will buy them, have a milder, sweeter flavour, though they are used in the same way. I remember when I was a teenager, local farmers used to approach my brothers and me, offering to pay us to help them pull up the huge roots. It was quite dangerous work as snakes used to come out the ground after the tractor had turned the earth but it was worth it for the money we pocketed.

Liquorice powder has the strongest, most concentrated flavour, and is also the sweetest. It can be used in small quantities in marinades or stirred directly into confectionery, custards and ice creams. The liqueur, made by infusing the roots in alcohol, produces an intensively flavoured digestive drink, which can also be used in marinades or sweets. Again, it is quite strong and should be used sparingly but it brings potent bitter and sweet backnotes.

The best liquorice in Calabria comes from Rossano. The Amarelli family have been harvesting liquorice since the sixteenth century. The production methods have been updated but the process of root selection, juice extraction, boiling and reduction still takes place in the original eighteenth-century factory, where the *maestro liquirizaio* (master liquorice maker) continues to supervise every batch to ensure that the paste is solidified at exactly the right temperature, thus maintaining the quality for which the family became famous.

Liquorice is generally considered a 'sweet' flavour but in Calabria we're proud to have taken it out of the realms of dessert and use it in savoury contexts, as a marinade for game (see page 172), duck, and even with fish (see page 120). As a punchy flavour liquorice works best with other strong flavours, such as mint, orange, bergamot, anise seeds and chilli, which will kick back. Calabrians also make a pasta with liquorice, but I confess I'm not really keen on it; I prefer liquorice to lift and work with other flavours, rather than be the star of the dish. Having said that, one of my favourite desserts is liquorice ice cream – the neutral background of the custard tempers the liquorice but still allows it to shine.

TARTUFO DI PIZZO

TARTUFO ICE CREAM 'MELTING HEARTS' from the town of Pizzo are something of a legend in Calabria. They are thought to have been invented in 1952 when a relation of the king came to celebrate a wedding in the town. The hosts did not have enough bowls to serve the ice cream, so a creative pastry maker, Don Pippo de Maria, decided to invent a way to serve the ice cream on plates instead. He cupped a layer of hazelnut then chocolate ice cream in his hand, poured in some melted chocolate then wrapped the ice creams up in paper to mould them before re-freezing them. Don Pippo's ice cream parlour is still in Pizzo's piazza and you can go and buy *tartufo*, made to his original recipe, still wrapped in paper.

Making *tartufo* yourself takes a little bit of time but it's something you can prepare in advance and is a great dessert for serving to friends as the large balls, dusted in cocoa powder to look like a big French truffle, are an impressive sight. Then you've got the added bonus of the first bite – dig your spoon in and the liquid chocolate centre runs out. It's a fantastically indulgent dessert and lots of fun.

If you want to shortcut the preparation you can buy good-quality chocolate and hazelnut (or another flavour) of ice cream, allow it to melt a little and then assemble the *tartufo* as directed.

MAKES 6

1 batch of Chocolate Ice Cream *(see page 240)*
1 batch of Hazelnut Ice Cream *(see page 241)*
cocoa powder, *to dust*

FOR THE CHOCOLATE SAUCE
85ml water
40g caster sugar
40g liquid glucose
90g double cream
30g cocoa powder
50g dark chocolate *(70 per cent cocoa solids), roughly broken into pieces*

FOR THE SUGARED HAZELNUTS
50g skinned hazelnuts
25ml water
50g caster sugar

First, make the ice creams if you're making your own.

Next, make the chocolate sauce. In a pan, bring the water, sugar, liquid glucose and double cream to a boil.

Remove from the heat and gradually stir in the cocoa powder. Return the pan to the heat and bring back to the boil, whisking continuously, then remove from the heat and gradually stir in the chocolate. Leave to cool, then place in the fridge until ready to use.

Line two trays with baking paper. Heat the oven to 200°C/fan 180°C/gas mark 6. In one tray, toast the hazelnuts for 8–10 minutes or until dark brown. In the meantime put the water into a small pan followed by the sugar (do not mix) and place on a high heat.

Bring the syrup to 140°C and add the hazelnuts straight from the oven. Mix rapidly on the heat until the sugar becomes dry and like sand. Remove from the heat, tip out onto the other prepared baking tray and set aside to cool.

If you're using shop-bought ice creams, take them out to soften a little.

To assemble, line six 100ml ramekins with square sheets of baking parchment, allowing some excess paper to hang over the sides. It's easier to do this if you scrunch it up first.

Put one large spoonful of chocolate ice cream in the lined ramekin and create a well. In the well, put two of the sugared hazelnuts and one spoonful of chocolate sauce. Cover the well with one spoonful of hazelnut ice cream making sure all the gaps are filled. Cover the hazelnut ice cream with more chocolate ice cream, enough to cover the hazelnut ice cream completely.

Fold up the excess paper to cover the ice cream and freeze again for 1–2 hours, or for 30 minutes if you like quite a soft ice cream.

Take out of the mould and unfold the paper to reveal the ice cream but leave the paper still attached to the bottom. Put on a plate and dust the top of the ice cream with a thick layer of cocoa powder.

GELATI

ICE CREAMS

I'M AFRAID THERE'S NO DEBATE, Italians are quite simply the masters of ice cream and we are the only nation to understand the recipe. A good, authentic Italian *gelato* will be soft and smooth without big ice crystals, which impair the flavour and make the ice cream watery. The fat content in a *gelato* also means it won't melt as quickly as other nations' interpretations.

Ice cream is held in such high regard in Italy that there is a whole ritual surrounding it. On Saturdays and Sundays, the post-lunch *passeggiata* (the early evening stroll) which culminates in a visit to the *gelateria* can become the main social event of the day, and whole families will take to the streets. In my family, we would all have to get dressed up before we set out, and this is still the case for many families today. If you're not expecting it, it can be quite a strange sight!

What follows are a couple of classic *gelati* flavours – rich and indulgent chocolate and hazelnut – but I have also included a recipe for one of my favourite flavours, coffee and anise. It's based on the Italian tradition of drinking an espresso, then cleaning your cup with a shot of Sambuca.

GELATO AL CIOCCOLATO

CHOCOLATE ICE CREAM

MAKES ABOUT 750ML

500ml full-fat milk
25g skimmed milk powder
125g caster sugar
175g dark chocolate *(70 per cent cocoa solids), roughly broken into pieces*
2 medium egg yolks

Stir the milk, milk powder and sugar together in a saucepan. Place over a medium heat and bring to a simmer, whisking regularly to prevent the mixture sticking to the bottom of the pan, then remove from the heat.

Add the chocolate and stir until melted and fully combined. Add the egg yolks and stir thoroughly with a whisk. Pass the mixture through a sieve to remove any lumps.

Transfer to the fridge to chill, then churn in an ice-cream machine following the manufacturer's instructions.

GELATO ALLA NOCIOLA

HAZELNUT ICE CREAM

MAKES ABOUT 600ML

500ml full-fat milk
25g skimmed milk powder
125g caster sugar
65g finely ground hazelnuts *(toast them in the oven at 200ºC/fan 180ºC/gas 6 for 8–10 minutes until coloured, process while still hot – add some milk if you need to)*
2 medium egg yolks

Stir the milk, milk powder and sugar together in a saucepan. Place over a medium heat and bring to a simmer, whisking regularly to prevent the mixture sticking to the bottom of the pan, then remove from the heat.

Add the finely ground hazelnuts and egg yolks and stir well. Blend the mixture with a hand blender, then pass through a sieve to remove any lumps.

Transfer to the fridge to chill, then churn in an ice-cream machine following the manufacturer's instructions.

GELATO CAFFÈ E ANICE

COFFEE ANISE ICE CREAM

MAKES ABOUT 700ML

1 tbsp whole coffee beans
500ml full-fat milk
10g ground coffee granules *(not instant coffee)*
125g caster sugar
25g skimmed milk powder
2 medium egg yolks
1 egg white
2 tsp Sambuca

Lightly crush the coffee beans with a rolling pin using a pestle and mortar.

Bring the milk to the boil and add the crushed coffee beans and ground coffee. Turn off the heat and leave to infuse for 10 minutes.

Strain the liquid and place back on a medium heat.

Whisk together the sugar, milk powder, egg yolks and whites in a bowl until combined. Add half the milk to the egg mixture and whisk quickly. When thoroughly combined, return the mixture to the pan with the rest of the milk; this prevents the eggs scrambling. Place back on the heat and whisk continuously until the mixture thickens to a custard thick enough to coat the back of a spoon, then remove from the heat, pass through a sieve into a bowl and chill in the fridge.

Once cold, stir in the Sambuca and churn in an ice-cream machine according to the manufacturer's instructions.

SORBETTI

SORBETS

THE WORD SORBET comes from the Arab word *sharbet*, meaning sweet snow, which is fitting because when I was a child my *nonna* used to mix coffee and sugar with fresh snow – like a coffee sorbet. Snow was a rare sight in Calabria so it was a fun way for us to play with it and have something sweet at the same time. The modern version, which is derived from the Roman practice of mixing ice with fruit and honey, is of course far more sophisticated but the idea is the same. The *cucina povera* philosophy meant that historically in the South we ate *granite* rather than *sorbetti*, which are a simpler, more rustic type of fruit and ice mixture, but I've included a small selection of sorbets here as it was a sorbet that really launched my career as a chef so they're something that are very personal to me and hold a special place in my heart and in my repertoire.

SORBETTO AL CAMPARI E ARANCIA ROSSA

BLOOD ORANGE AND CAMPARI SORBET

SERVES 8 (MAKES ABOUT 600ML)

200ml water
180g caster sugar
grated zest of 2 blood oranges
100g liquid glucose
225ml blood orange juice *(you'll need around 4 oranges)*
50ml Campari

Put the water, sugar, orange zest and liquid glucose into a pan and heat gently to dissolve the sugar. Bring to the boil, then pass the liquid through a sieve into a bowl. Chill.

Once cold, mix the syrup with the orange juice and Campari and churn in an ice-cream machine following the manufacturer's instructions until frozen.

SORBETTO DI FRAGOLE

STRAWBERRY SORBET

SERVES 6 (MAKES AROUND 500ML)

200g hulled strawberries
120ml water
240g Sorbet Syrup *(see below)*
20ml lemon juice

FOR THE SORBET SYRUP

70g caster sugar
40g liquid glucose
125ml water

First, put all the ingredients for the sorbet syrup into a small pan and bring to the boil. Remove from the heat and set aside to cool completely.

Whizz the strawberries in a small blender to make a smooth sauce. When the syrup is completely cold, stir in the blended strawberries, water and lemon juice. Churn in an ice-cream machine following the manufacturer's instructions until frozen.

SORBETTO DI LIMONI

LEMON SORBET

SERVES 10 (MAKES ABOUT 800ML)

210g caster sugar
100g liquid glucose
450ml water
pared zest of 2 lemons
200ml lemon juice *(you'll need 5 or 6 juicy lemons)*

Mix together all the ingredients except the lemon juice in a pan and bring to the boil.

As soon as the mixture starts to boil, remove from the heat, pass through a sieve (discard the pared zest) and set aside to cool.

When it's completely cold, stir in the lemon juice then churn in an ice-cream machine following the manufacturer's instructions until frozen.

A NOTE ABOUT MAKING BREAD

BAKING BREAD IS A WONDERFUL THING TO DO and the joy of putting a home-made loaf on the table is infinite, but I'm aware that it does take time and is therefore not something that I, or many people, can realistically do every day. But because bread is a lifeblood in the South, no book on southern Italian food would be complete without at least a few recipes for the breads we put on our table at every single meal.

What follows are recipes for breads that are simply favourites of mine, or that I consider particularly southern – pizza was invented in Campania, don't forget – and that you will be sure to find in homes throughout the *mezzogiorno* region. There's no denying that several of the breads are for the enthusiast; for those of you that want to spend a bit of time laying the groundwork for bread-making and then enjoying an afternoon or even a day creating your loaf. That said, there are a couple – the *freselle* on page 254 and the *taralli* on page 260 – that are easier to throw together and, most importantly, because they're crisp breads they will keep for several days.

The groundwork for the larger loaves begins about 10 days or so before you can bake your bread. You will need to make a 'starter', and for my recipe, the starter is in fact made in two stages (see page 253).

The main flour I've used in these recipes is '00' flour. In Italy I'd use a stronger flour, either a '0' or a '0' Manitoba flour (made from a variety of hard wheat), but here in the UK those aren't easy to come by and '00' works well. Your bread crust will perhaps be slightly softer than bread as I'd find it at home, but this flour has the advantage of proving more quickly than the stronger ones.

I use fresh yeast rather than dried because I think there is a subtle flavour difference between the two and I prefer the slight sweetness that the fresh yeast yields, but I know some people can't taste any difference. Fresh yeast isn't hard to find – most health food shops stock it, as well as some larger supermarkets, and if you're lucky enough to have a local baker, they should be able to provide you with a small quantity, which is all you need. The breads will work just as well with dried yeast, however, and I've given you the measurements and instructions for using it too.

I've given you approximate timings for how long you will need to let your loaves prove (rise) but the time it takes depends on the temperature of the room in which you leave your bread, and how active your yeast is. It's really a case of getting a feel for it and of waiting until your dough has doubled in size. The more you bake bread, the more you will come to understand when it's ready.

LIEVITI

STARTERS

A STARTER IS THE FOUNDATION OF YOUR DOUGH. It is what gives your bread its texture and flavour and even dictates how chewy your crust will be. A starter is created by mixing flour and water. Left in the open, the combination mixes with the air in your kitchen or fridge to create wild yeast spores, which multiply and ferment and add acidity to your bread's flavour and create its strong texture. Once made, you need to keep the yeast spores in the starter alive by 'feeding' them every day. Don't worry, though, it's something that takes a few minutes and once you've got into the habit, it will become like second nature and you can keep your starter alive forever.

My starter has two stages: first, you make a 'mother yeast', an extra strong yeast, which helps boost the starter and gives your bread the power it needs to rise. Then you make the main *levato* (starter). *Levato* means to 'stand up' and that's what the second starter is doing – it lifts the bread, helping it to rise further and form its beautiful holes.

I know this might all sound a bit time-consuming and laborious, but it's not complicated to do. I believe that a loaf is something you should be proud of, and for that, it's really worth investing a bit of time upfront.

LIEVITO MADRE

MOTHER YEAST

150g '00' flour
150g water

Mix the flour and water and place in a bowl.

Leave in the fridge, uncovered, for 5 days. After this time a crust will have formed. Remove the crust, mix the yeast well and leave for 2 days.

The yeast can now be fed each day, adding equal amounts of flour and water to it every day, and it will keep for years!

LEVATO

BREAD STARTER

300g Mother Yeast
300g '00' flour
250g water

Mix the ingredients together and use as directed in your recipe.

FRESELLE

FRESELLE ARE A PUGLIAN CRISP BREAD. They're half-baked, removed from the oven and sliced in half, then returned to the oven and allowed to bake again until crisp. The result is something that could crack your teeth (almost).

Freselle are a versatile bread. They make wonderful bruschetta so pile them high with all kinds of toppings – for breakfast, lunch or dinner; but I also love them as a deconstructed salad, broken up and stirred through a bowl of tomato and mozzarella salad dressed with olive oil, where they will absorb all the juices and flavours and become a soft, spongy bread – absolutely beautiful. You can find different shapes of *freselle* but the ring shapes shown in the photo are the most common.

MAKES ABOUT 12

250g '00' flour, *plus extra for dusting*
50g rye flour
225ml lukewarm water
125g Bread Starter *(see page 253)*
10g salt
olive oil, *for greasing*

Mix together the flours and lukewarm water in a bowl and leave to rest for 1 hour.

Mix in the starter and salt. Turn the dough out on to a clean kitchen surface and knead for 10 minutes until the dough is smooth. Put the dough into a lightly oiled bowl, cover with a damp tea towel and let it rise for 2½–3 hours.

Preheat the oven to 220°C/fan 200°C/gas 7. Line two large baking trays with baking paper.

Divide the dough into 12 even-sized pieces and roll into balls using a little flour if the dough is very sticky. Transfer to the baking trays, and leave to prove for 20 minutes or until doubled in size.

Dip the end of a wooden spoon in flour and push it down into the middle of each ball. Pull the hole outwards to make a hole about 6–7cm wide, then flatten the breads until they are about 2cm high.

Bake in the oven for 12 minutes. Take the breads out, slice each one in half horizontally and return to the oven for another 25–30 minutes until they've turned a dark golden brown. Remove from the oven and leave to cool on a wire rack. The freselle will keep for up to a week in an airtight tin.

PANE DI CERCHIARA

CERCHIARA BREAD

CERCHIARA IS THE TOWN WHERE I WAS BORN and it has become famous around Italy for its eponymous bread. Nowadays, most families will buy their bread from a bakery, but when I was growing up families made bread at home. The responsibility for bread-making was split and the *levato* was passed from family to family for each to take their turn. The family kept the starter for a week, baking each day and sharing out the bread between the homes. I remember the *levato* my family shared was kept in a small white container with a tea towel over the top and I used to see the women carrying it between households, like a baby. There was a huge amount of superstition around the *levato* and it was a disaster for the community if it died. It's funny because although the breads were all made from the same starter, each family used to produce a different flavour of bread.

Traditional Cerchiara loaves typically weigh between 2 and 3kg each but they can weigh up to 10kg, so while there are many *panificio* (bakeries) in Cerchiara, only three still sell the very large loaves and send them out to shops around the whole country. The bread takes time to make and such huge quantities of dough require somebody with strong arms, but once made a loaf can stay fresh for up to 10 days if kept in paper bags. Then, in the *cucina povera* tradition, after the 10 days, it can still be used and has different uses at each stage of its life. As it starts to become a little stale, the centre will be hollowed out and grated to make breadcrumbs, then when it's very dry the crust can be soaked in soup to bulk it out into a meal.

My brother Valerio created the recipe here. It is an adaptation of the traditional one, using the principles and ingredients of the original, but the finished loaf is much smaller and the process has been simplified. It might take a bit of practice to get it perfect but if you're into your bread-making it's well worth a shot. Don't eat your bread the day it's made – it will be too warm and gluey in the middle. Start enjoying it the next day and store it in a large brown paper bag (in restaurants we use the sacks the flour comes in), or wrap it in a clean tea towel.

800g '00' flour
200g rye flour
300g Mother Yeast *(see page 253)*
750–825ml water
20g salt

In a very large bowl, mix all the ingredients together. Start with the lower quantity of water and if the dough looks as though it needs a bit more moisture to make it smooth and stretchy, add more. Leave the dough to rest until doubled in size – it will take at least 2 hours, depending on the warmth of the room.

Preheat your oven to 220°C/fan 200°C/gas 9. Remove the dough from the bowl, shape it into a round, then lay your arm across the middle of the dough and fold it over, which will create the bread's characteristic 'rasella' – the bulge on the side (there's a photo of it on page 186), then transfer it to a large baking sheet or oven tray.

Bake for 1 hour 25 minutes, then turn the oven down to 170°C/fan 150°C/gas 3 and bake for another 1 hour 25 minutes. Switch the oven off and leave the bread inside to cool – it will take about 4½ hours. You should now have a beautiful dark crust and a loaf with a strong texture and plenty of holes inside.

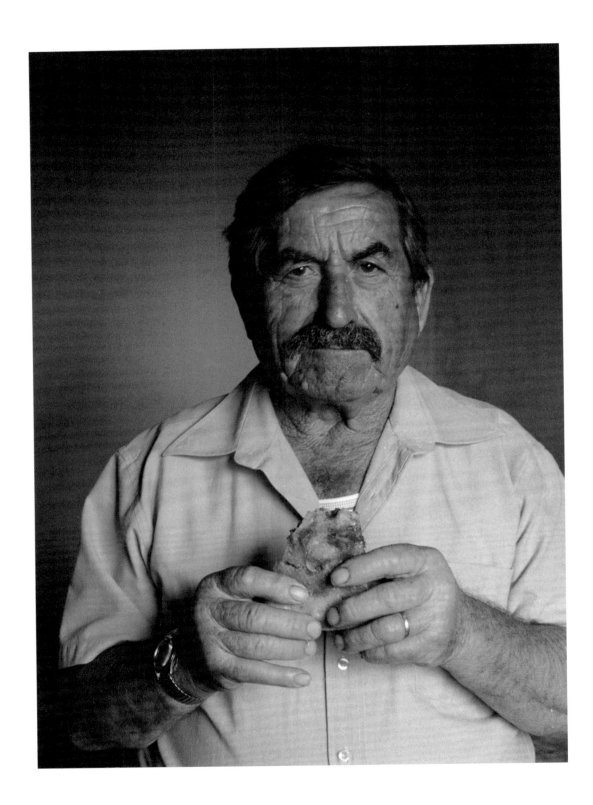

TARALLI

TARALLI ARE A SOUTHERN SNACK FOOD – a very dry, crunchy, crisp bread, generally savoury, though sometimes sweet. In savoury form, they're spiced with a hint of fennel seeds and sometimes, as here, enriched with white wine. Because they're so dry, *taralli* are best dipped in liquid, and if you go for a beer or glass of wine with friends at *aperitivo* time you will more than likely be given a bowl of *taralli* for dipping in your drink – I am a big fan of dunking them in my red wine. Many traditional southern recipes use lard in the dough, which gives a richer flavour, but olive oil is just as good.

MAKES ABOUT 40
Depending what size or shape you make

250g '00' flour
5g fine salt
20ml white wine
5g lard or olive oil
½ tsp fennel seeds
25g Mother Yeast *(see page 253)*
125 ml water

Preheat the oven to 260°C / fan 240°C / gas 9.

Place all the ingredients except the water in the bowl of a stand mixer fitted with the dough hook. Use your hands to combine them, then turn the machine on to a slow speed and add the water. Mix for about 5 minutes, until a dough has formed.

Remove the dough from the bowl, and divide it into about six pieces. Place a piece on a board or worktop and use your fingers to roll each piece into a long thin rope, about 1cm in diameter.

Cut into pieces of 5–40cm in length, depending on how big you want your taralli, then roll each out a little thinner. Make a ring or knot shape then seal the join with water. Repeat with the remaining ropes.

Bring a large saucepan of water to the boil and add a few of the shaped taralli, and leave them until they float, then remove with a slotted spoon and place on a tea towel to drain. Repeat until they have all been boiled.

Place the taralli on baking trays greased with olive oil and bake for about 12–15 minutes, until golden brown.

OLIO EXTRA VIRGINE DI OLIVA

EXTRA VIRGIN OLIVE OIL

ITALY HAS BEEN PRODUCING OLIVE OIL since around the seventh century BC, and even then it was revered by the Greeks and Romans for its health properties and power to heal wounds. Today it is still the world's second largest producer, after Spain, and 18 of Italy's 20 regions grow olives – hundreds of varieties. For most Italians, olive oil is as essential to their diet as pasta and good vegetables, or put another way as intrinsic to our way of eating as butter is to the French. Climate is the main influence on production, so within Italy around 80 per cent of the total output comes from the South, mainly Calabria, Puglia and Sicily. There are some excellent oils from Umbria and the North – particularly in Liguria, Tuscany and the Lake Garda area, but the irascibility of the climate means that production is very limited compared to the *mezzogiorno*.

In the South, it is the long, dry, warm summers, mild winters and the soil – not too fertile, not too dry – which means that great swathes of the land mass is given over to olive groves. Given the olive tree's noble status and legendary reputation, there is nothing particularly remarkable about the trees themselves – the leaves have no strong fragrance and the tangled branches of trees are not great beauties. But for an Italian there is something emotive about their appearance, which evokes health, vitality and a sense of one's home. It is also the volume that is most striking. There are hillsides in Calabria, Puglia and Sicily where all you can see for miles around are the twisted branches of the trees.

ITALY IS THE WORLD'S SECOND LARGEST PRODUCER OF OLIVE OIL AND 18 OF ITALY'S 20 REGIONS GROW OLIVES

The period for harvesting olives is October to November, depending on the region. For the best olive oil, the fruits need to be picked from the tree by hand – the more gently the olives are treated, the better the oil, so they mustn't be left to fall. There are various types of machine that shake the trees, but the best producers would argue the quality of the oil suffers.

Once harvested, the olives are pressed to extract their juice. Extra virgin olive oil is the highest quality and most expensive type of oil and must come from the first pressing. But to earn its 'extra virgin' label the oil still has to pass several other taste, aroma and acidity tests. The taste tests assess how fruity, peppery and bitter the oil is, while the acidity test assesses its percentage of oleic acid. To be classed as 'extra virgin' an oil must have less than 0.8 per cent oleic acid, making it the least acidic of any oil. The next grades – virgin olive oil, olive oil and then various other types of refined oils (tainted by some kind of chemicals) are similarly graded.

Among families and farmers, the first pressing of the oil is a big event and everyone gathers round to assess the flavour. The freshly pressed *verdone* is a bright green, cloudy oil. It's quite shocking when you see it for the first time – in a good way – and the taste is absolutely fantastic. A drizzle added to a *pasta e fagioli* (see page 74) or over mozzarella is amazing. The oil stays like that for up to three days, then the sediment settles and you have to pour the oil into a different bottle. The colour and punchy, fresh flavour last for a couple of weeks, which is why *verdone* stays in Italy and you generally have to know somebody to experience it. It's often given as gifts and it's a real honour to receive such treasured nectar.

You might hear people say that you should use extra virgin oil only for salads and dressings as the flavour is too strong and peppery for cooking, but if I could afford it, I would use extra virgin olive oil for everything: frying, roasting, marinades. If you think that every region, every type of olive, even every hill produces its own

FOR THE BEST OIL, THE OLIVES NEED TO BE PICKED FROM THE TREE BY HAND

flavour of oil, then if you choose one that suits your taste, an extra virgin oil – the highest quality, purest kind – can suit every purpose.

I like my olive oil mild – not very peppery; not very strong. In Italy we have a wonderful custom of dipping bread in oil before a meal, allowing you to experience the oil's flavour almost as unadulterated as it can be. But such is the potency of olive oil, that if the oil is too grassy, very bitter, too strong or too pungent, that taste will linger on your palate and it can destroy your whole meal by killing your ability to taste more gentle flavours.

Most Italians buy their oil directly from a local producer or from someone they know; the big brands generally export theirs. I'm still lucky enough to buy mine from the area around my family home. It's pressed from mild

Cassanese olives and the trees were planted by my grandmother. These days, it's very time-consuming and a lot of hard work to harvest the olives and press the oils ourselves, so a *frantoio* – the man who owns all the necessary machinery

IF I COULD AFFORD IT, I WOULD USE EXTRA VIRGIN OLIVE OIL FOR EVERYTHING: FRYING, ROASTING AND MARINADES

– comes and harvests the olives from our trees for us. He then presses the oil, we take half of it and he takes half to sell as he wishes. It's a happy arrangement and means that the oil still has the strong family and emotional connections for me. I couldn't cook with anything else.

When it comes to buying yours, it's really a matter of what suits your taste so my best advice would be to try different types of olive and producer. Olive oil doesn't age well so you really need to be buying it from this year's harvest – most bottles should now indicate this. And don't worry about colour; oil can come in all different shades, from straw yellow to grassy green.

PIZZA MARGHERITA

WHERE WOULD NAPLES BE WITHOUT PIZZA? Or rather, where would the world be without pizza? One of Campania's most famous exports has become a worldwide favourite and that makes me so proud. You can eat some fantastic authentic Italian pizza in restaurants around the UK, but there is something fun and unique about making your own at home, and if you've got kids it's such a great opportunity to get them involved in cooking, even if it's just to choose their topping. By 'authentic' Italian, I mean a very thin, crisp crust (not a thick doughy one), and with a topping that's not drowning in tomato sauce, but lightly coated in it so the dough and other toppings can still shine.

If you've got time, I really would urge you to let your dough prove overnight in the fridge. It will develop acidity, like a sourdough bread, and will have an amazing crust.

This recipe is of course just a guide. Play with your toppings; make a *calzone* (folded pizza); make *pizza bianco* (using crème fraîche as the base instead of tomatoes); and use the dough to make *puccia* (see page 58).

MAKES 4

FOR THE DOUGH
225g '00' flour, *plus extra for dusting*
225g strong bread flour
7g fresh yeast or 3g fast-action dried yeast
15g salt
250–300ml water

FOR THE TOPPING
1 × 400g can peeled plum tomatoes
1 tsp dried oregano
3 tbsp extra virgin olive oil
2 mozzarella balls, *about 125–150g each*
handful of basil leaves
40g Grana Padano cheese
sea salt and freshly ground black pepper

For the dough, mix the flours, yeast and salt together in a large mixing bowl. Gradually add the water, mixing well to form a soft dough. Turn the dough out on to a floured work surface and knead for about five minutes, until smooth and elastic. Transfer to a clean bowl, cover with a damp tea towel and leave to rise for about 1½ hours, or until doubled in size (ideally leave it overnight).

When the dough has risen, knock it back (punch the air out), then knead again until smooth. Roll into a ball and set aside for 30 minutes to 1 hour, or until it doubles in size again. The time it takes to prove will depend on the temperature in your kitchen; the warmer the place, the quicker the prove.

Meanwhile, prepare the topping. Pass the tomato through a vegetable mill. Add the oregano and oil, season with salt and pepper and set aside. Alternatively put the ingredients into a mini food processor and blend until smooth.

Preheat the oven to 250°C / fan 230°C / gas 9. Divide the dough into four balls and roll each out on a lightly floured work surface until 20–30cm in diameter and about 5mm thick. Spread the tomato sauce all over each pizza base. Cut or tear the mozzarella in rough slices and finish with basil leaves and some shavings of the Grana Padano.

Lightly flour a baking sheet(s) with '00' flour. Bake the pizzas (you will have to cook them in batches) for about 8–10 minutes, depending on the thickness, until the base is crispy. Finish with more basil leaves.

FOCACCIA OLIVE E ACCIUGE

YOU WILL FIND FOCACCIA ALL OVER ITALY, but this version, which has been developed with my brother Valerio, tops the bread with olives and anchovies and is a particularly southern combination. It reminds me of the Sicilian *pane cunzato* (dressed bread) which is eaten as a mid-morning snack.

SERVES 8—10

FOR THE POOLISH STARTER
250g '00' flour
2.5g fresh yeast or 1g dried active yeast
275g water

FOR THE DOUGH
7g fresh yeast or 3g dried active yeast
155ml warm water
425g '00' flour
70ml olive oil
15g salt

FOR THE TOPPING
20ml olive oil
20ml water
coarse sea salt
50g pitted black olives
10 anchovy fillets
dried oregano

Make the poolish starter the day before by combining the flour, yeast and the water in a large bowl. Mix well with a spoon then cover and leave in a warm place overnight.

The next day, put the yeast into a bowl and stir in half the water. Set aside to allow the yeast to activate. Sift the flour into a large bowl (or the bowl of a stand mixer fitted with a dough hook) and stir in the olive oil and salt. Make a well in the middle and add the remaining water, then pour in the activated yeast mixture. Add the poolish starter to the mixture, too.

Mix everything together well and then knead the dough on a board for about 10–15 minutes if kneading by hand or 8–10 minutes if using a mixer. Put the dough back into a clean, oiled bowl and cover and leave to rise for 3–4 hours or until the dough has doubled in size.

Tip the dough out onto a board and roll out into a rough oval shape about 2cm thick. Transfer to an oiled baking tray, at least 5cm deep, and stretch and press down on the dough to fill the tray, then push your fingers down all over the surface to 'pit' the surface with holes.

Cover with a tea towel and set aside to prove again for 45 minutes to 1 hour, or until doubled in size. Preheat the oven to 240°C / fan 220°C / gas 9.

Drizzle the top of the bread with the oil, sprinkle over the water and some sea salt, then push the olives and anchovies into the top of the dough before scattering over the oregano. Bake in the oven for about 25 minutes until golden or the loaf sounds hollow when tapped on top. Transfer to a wire rack and leave to cool before slicing or tearing.

8
SALSE E
CONDIMENTI

SALSA DI POMODORO

TOMATO SAUCE

THERE'S NO SECRET TO MAKING a great Italian tomato sauce: you need to use tomatoes at the peak of their ripeness and cook them right down, adding as little liquid as possible at the beginning so that your sauce is thick and rich. This will give you a beautiful concentrated tomato flavour and you can then thin the sauce to the consistency you want. Adding a little of the starchy water from cooking pasta is the best way to do this – it loosens the sauce but also gives it wonderful body and creaminess.

You'll quickly discover that this sauce is a pillar of many recipes in this book, used in the pasta and meat dishes, in particular, so it's worth making the full quantity and freezing what you don't need. It will keep well in the fridge for a few days or in the freezer for 2–3 weeks.

MAKES ABOUT 775ML

300g white onion, *very finely sliced*
4 tbsp extra virgin olive oil
1kg ripe good-flavoured tomatoes *(preferably on the vine)*, *roughly chopped*
2 garlic cloves, *chopped*
20g basil leaves
sea salt

Put the onion into a saucepan with half the oil and let it sweat slowly over a low–medium heat for around 15 minutes until it's soft (do not allow it to colour). If it looks as though it might catch, add a splash of water to the pan.

Add the tomatoes and season with salt. Leave to simmer over a low heat for about 45 minutes, until the tomatoes are thick and rich, adding a little water if the level of the liquid gets too low. Remove from the heat.

Put the remaining oil in another pan with the garlic and cook over a low–medium heat. When it's almost golden brown, add the basil leaves and stir. Pass the oil through a sieve into the cooked tomato sauce.

Whisk the sauce to break up the tomatoes. If it's too thick, thin it with a little water, ideally some pasta cooking water. Pass the sauce through a wide-holed sieve resting over a bowl, and use the back of a ladle to extract the smooth mixture. Check the seasoning and add more salt if necessary.

SALSA AL BASILICO

BASIL SAUCE

I KNOW YOU'RE THINKING THIS IS ESSENTIALLY A PESTO, but I can assure you it's not. Firstly, there are no pine nuts, which means it has a smoother consistency, and I blanch the basil leaves before blending them with the other ingredients, which keeps their lovely bright colour (pesto can be very dark) and gives the sauce a milder, less pungent basil flavour. It's a lively, fresh sauce that's great with grilled fish or steamed prawns. Swap the basil for parsley or chervil for a change.

MAKES ABOUT 200ML

75g basil leaves
15g Grana Padano cheese
7g pecorino cheese
small slice of a garlic clove
125ml extra virgin olive oil
sea salt and freshly ground black pepper

Pick the leaves of the basil, then place in a colander and pour over boiling water to blanch. Transfer the leaves to a bowl of iced water to cool, then drain.

Put all the ingredients and about 50ml of the oil in a blender. Start to blend and continue to add more oil slowly, until you have a creamy paste.

Check the seasoning and adjust the salt and pepper. The sauce will keep for 2–3 days in the fridge, no longer.

MARMELLATA DI PEPERONCINI

CHILLI JAM

THIS RECIPE WAS BORN FROM the fact that in Calabria we have an abundance of chillies; more than we can find meals for, so the British practice of cooking fruit and vegetables down into jams or chutneys to preserve them is a perfect way to make sure they don't go to waste. I'd serve this as a dip for calamari or deep-fried courgette flowers (see page 202) but it would also add an interesting dimension to a cheese board.

MAKES ABOUT 800—900G

1kg red pepper, *deseeded and finely chopped*
260g red chillies, *deseeded and finely chopped*
6g Thai red chilli *(about 6), deseeded and finely chopped*
500g caster sugar
125ml red wine
125ml red wine vinegar
85ml clear honey
½ tsp fine sea salt

Place the peppers and chillies in a pan with the remaining ingredients and bring to the boil. Cover the surface of the liquid with a circle of baking paper and cook for 1 hour over the lowest heat possible.

Remove the paper cover from the pan, check the liquid level and continue to cook gently for 10–15 minutes until you have a jam-like consistency. It will firm up as it cools, so take care not to overcook it at this stage. Leave to cool then transfer to a lidded container until ready to use. You can store it in the fridge for up to two weeks.

MARMELLATA DI CIPOLLA ROSSA

RED ONION JAM

THE TROPEA ONION SEASON is short – just a few months – but we can never use them as quickly as they grow so cooking large quantities and reducing them to jam is a great way to preserve them. Serve this with any soft cheese – it's particularly good with burrata; steamed or grilled meat; or spread it on bruschetta with ricotta. It's got just the right balance of acidity and sweetness to cope with a range of flavours.

MAKES ABOUT 800G

1kg red Tropea onions or normal red onions,
   finely sliced
150g caster sugar
150g clear honey
120ml red wine vinegar

Place the onions, sugar, honey and 20ml of the vinegar in a large deep pan over a very low heat and allow to cook for approximately 2 hours covered with a lid.

When the water from the onions has completely evaporated, add the remaining vinegar and simmer until the jam has reached your desired consistency. I serve this as quite a thick but still slightly running jam, which is great for cheese.

Allow to cool then transfer to a lidded container until ready to use. You can store the jam in the fridge for up to two weeks.

INDEX

Page references in *italics* indicate photographs.

LIST OF STOCKISTS

ONLINE

www.melburyandappleton.co.uk (fantastic general supplier for all Italian ingredients)
www.natoora.co.uk (particularly good for fruit and vegetables)
www.thedrinkshop.com (for liquorice liqueur)
www.bakerybits.co.uk (for a range of flours and bread-baking equipment)

DELICATESSENS

Chandos Deli
Various branches in Bristol, Bath and Exeter
www.chandosdeli.com

I Camisa & Son
61 Old Compton Street
London W1D 6HS
www.icamisa.co.uk

Gazzano's
167–9 Farringdon Road
London EC1R 3AL

Lina Stores (they also have an online shop)
18 Brewer Street
London W1F 0SH
www.linastores.co.uk

Valentina Fine Foods
Various branches around London and the South East, with an online shop too
www.valentinafinefoods.com

Valvona & Crolla (they also have an online shop)
19 Elm Row
Edinburgh EH7 4AA
www.valvonacrolla.co.uk